REER EXAMINATION SERIES

D0796583

THIS IS YOUR **PASSBOOK**® FOR ...

CUSTODIAN

NLC®

NATIONAL LEARNING CORPORATION®

passbooks.com

COPYRIGHT NOTICE

Copyright © 2018 by

NLC®

National Learning Corporation

212 Michael Drive, Syosset, NY 11791
(516) 921-8888 • www.passbooks.com
E-mail: info@passbooks.com

PUBLISHED IN THE UNITED STATES OF AMERICA

PASSBOOK® SERIES

THE *PASSBOOK® SERIES* has been created to prepare applicants and candidates for the ultimate academic battlefield – the examination room.

At some time in our lives, each and every one of us may be required to take an examination – for validation, matriculation, admission, qualification, registration, certification, or licensure.

Based on the assumption that every applicant or candidate has met the basic formal educational standards, has taken the required number of courses, and read the necessary texts, the *PASSBOOK® SERIES* furnishes the one special preparation which may assure passing with confidence, instead of failing with insecurity. Examination questions – together with answers – are furnished as the basic vehicle for study so that the mysteries of the examination and its compounding difficulties may be eliminated or diminished by a sure method.

This book is meant to help you pass your examination provided that you qualify and are serious in your objective.

The entire field is reviewed through the huge store of content information which is succinctly presented through a provocative and challenging approach – the question-and-answer method.

A climate of success is established by furnishing the correct answers at the end of each test.

You soon learn to recognize types of questions, forms of questions, and patterns of questioning. You may even begin to anticipate expected outcomes.

You perceive that many questions are repeated or adapted so that you can gain acute insights, which may enable you to score many sure points.

You learn how to confront new questions, or types of questions, and to attack them confidently and work out the correct answers.

You note objectives and emphases, and recognize pitfalls and dangers, so that you may make positive educational adjustments.

Moreover, you are kept fully informed in relation to new concepts, methods, practices, and directions in the field.

You discover that you arre actually taking the examination all the time: you are preparing for the examination by "taking" an examination, not by reading extraneous and/or supererogatory textbooks.

In short, this PASSBOOK®, used directedly, should be an important factor in helping you to pass your test.

CUSTODIAN

DUTIES:
Sweeps and mops floors and stairs; dusts desks, woodwork, furniture, and other equipment; washes windows, walls, blackboards, sinks, and other fixtures; polishes furniture and metal furnishings; empties waste baskets, collects and disposes of rubbish; clears snow and ice from walks and driveways; mows lawns; trims shrubs, rakes leaves, and performs a variety of other grounds keeping tasks; operates a coal or oil low pressure heating system including firing and removing ashes; delivers' packages and messages; checks operation of clocks and bells; puts out and takes in traffic safety signs; arranges chairs and tables and other equipment for special use of school building; repairs window shades, replaces light bulbs, soap and towels; paints rooms and equipment, repairs furniture, and makes minor plumbing, electrical, and carpentry repairs; prepares and maintains a variety of records and reports.

EXAMPLES OF WORK:
- Sweeps, mops, vacuums, and washes floors and stairs;
- Uses heavy mechanical equipment in stripping, waxing, and polishing floors;
- Dusts chairs, tables, desks, and other furniture;
- Polishes furniture and brass;
- Empties wastebaskets and collects and disposes of trash;
- Arranges chairs and tables and other equipment for special use of building;
- Repairs window shades, replaces light bulbs, soap, and towels;
- Moves furniture, supplies, and other equipment;
- Cleans walls, bath fixtures, equipment, and furniture;
- May clear snow and ice from walks;
- Mows lawns, trim shrubs, rakes leaves, and performs a variety of other groundskeeping tasks assigned;
- May assist in the operation and maintenance of an oil-or-gas-fired low-pressure heating system;
- Washes windows, walls, blackboards, sinks, and other fixtures;
- Makes minor plumbing, carpentry, painting, and electrical repairs;
- Prepares and maintains simple records and reports.

SCOPE OF THE WRITTEN EXAMINATION
The multiple-choice will cover knowledge, skills, and/or abilities in such areas as:
1. Building cleaning;
2. Building operation and simple building maintenance;
3. Cleaning tools and their uses; and
4. Health and safety issues in custodial work.

HOW TO TAKE A TEST

I. YOU MUST PASS AN EXAMINATION

A. WHAT EVERY CANDIDATE SHOULD KNOW

Examination applicants often ask us for help in preparing for the written test. What can I study in advance? What kinds of questions will be asked? How will the test be given? How will the papers be graded?

As an applicant for a civil service examination, you may be wondering about some of these things. Our purpose here is to suggest effective methods of advance study and to describe civil service examinations.

Your chances for success on this examination can be increased if you know how to prepare. Those "pre-examination jitters" can be reduced if you know what to expect. You can even experience an adventure in good citizenship if you know why civil service exams are given.

B. WHY ARE CIVIL SERVICE EXAMINATIONS GIVEN?

Civil service examinations are important to you in two ways. As a citizen, you want public jobs filled by employees who know how to do their work. As a job seeker, you want a fair chance to compete for that job on an equal footing with other candidates. The best-known means of accomplishing this two-fold goal is the competitive examination.

Exams are widely publicized throughout the nation. They may be administered for jobs in federal, state, city, municipal, town or village governments or agencies.

Any citizen may apply, with some limitations, such as the age or residence of applicants. Your experience and education may be reviewed to see whether you meet the requirements for the particular examination. When these requirements exist, they are reasonable and applied consistently to all applicants. Thus, a competitive examination may cause you some uneasiness now, but it is your privilege and safeguard.

C. HOW ARE CIVIL SERVICE EXAMS DEVELOPED?

Examinations are carefully written by trained technicians who are specialists in the field known as "psychological measurement," in consultation with recognized authorities in the field of work that the test will cover. These experts recommend the subject matter areas or skills to be tested; only those knowledges or skills important to your success on the job are included. The most reliable books and source materials available are used as references. Together, the experts and technicians judge the difficulty level of the questions.

Test technicians know how to phrase questions so that the problem is clearly stated. Their ethics do not permit "trick" or "catch" questions. Questions may have been tried out on sample groups, or subjected to statistical analysis, to determine their usefulness.

Written tests are often used in combination with performance tests, ratings of training and experience, and oral interviews. All of these measures combine to form the best-known means of finding the right person for the right job.

II. HOW TO PASS THE WRITTEN TEST

A. NATURE OF THE EXAMINATION

To prepare intelligently for civil service examinations, you should know how they differ from school examinations you have taken. In school you were assigned certain definite pages to read or subjects to cover. The examination questions were quite detailed and usually emphasized memory. Civil service exams, on the other hand, try to discover your present ability to perform the duties of a position, plus your potentiality to learn these duties. In other words, a civil service exam attempts to predict how successful you will be. Questions cover such a broad area that they cannot be as minute and detailed as school exam questions.

In the public service similar kinds of work, or positions, are grouped together in one "class." This process is known as *position-classification*. All the positions in a class are paid according to the salary range for that class. One class title covers all of these positions, and they are all tested by the same examination.

B. FOUR BASIC STEPS

1) Study the announcement

How, then, can you know what subjects to study? Our best answer is: "Learn as much as possible about the class of positions for which you've applied." The exam will test the knowledge, skills and abilities needed to do the work.

Your most valuable source of information about the position you want is the official exam announcement. This announcement lists the training and experience qualifications. Check these standards and apply only if you come reasonably close to meeting them.

The brief description of the position in the examination announcement offers some clues to the subjects which will be tested. Think about the job itself. Review the duties in your mind. Can you perform them, or are there some in which you are rusty? Fill in the blank spots in your preparation.

Many jurisdictions preview the written test in the exam announcement by including a section called "Knowledge and Abilities Required," "Scope of the Examination," or some similar heading. Here you will find out specifically what fields will be tested.

2) Review your own background

Once you learn in general what the position is all about, and what you need to know to do the work, ask yourself which subjects you already know fairly well and which need improvement. You may wonder whether to concentrate on improving your strong areas or on building some background in your fields of weakness. When the announcement has specified "some knowledge" or "considerable knowledge," or has used adjectives like "beginning principles of..." or "advanced ... methods," you can get a clue as to the number and difficulty of questions to be asked in any given field. More questions, and hence broader coverage, would be included for those subjects which are more important in the work. Now weigh your strengths and weaknesses against the job requirements and prepare accordingly.

3) Determine the level of the position

Another way to tell how intensively you should prepare is to understand the level of the job for which you are applying. Is it the entering level? In other words, is this the position in which beginners in a field of work are hired? Or is it an intermediate or advanced level? Sometimes this is indicated by such words as "Junior" or "Senior" in the class title. Other jurisdictions use Roman numerals to designate the level – Clerk I, Clerk II, for example. The word "Supervisor" sometimes appears in the title. If the level is not indicated by the title, check the description of duties. Will you be working under very close supervision, or will you have responsibility for independent decisions in this work?

4) Choose appropriate study materials

Now that you know the subjects to be examined and the relative amount of each subject to be covered, you can choose suitable study materials. For beginning level jobs, or even advanced ones, if you have a pronounced weakness in some aspect of your training, read a modern, standard textbook in that field. Be sure it is up to date and has general coverage. Such books are normally available at your library, and the librarian will be glad to help you locate one. For entry-level positions, questions of appropriate difficulty are chosen – neither highly advanced questions, nor those too simple. Such questions require careful thought but not advanced training.

If the position for which you are applying is technical or advanced, you will read more advanced, specialized material. If you are already familiar with the basic principles of your field, elementary textbooks would waste your time. Concentrate on advanced textbooks and technical periodicals. Think through the concepts and review difficult problems in your field.

These are all general sources. You can get more ideas on your own initiative, following these leads. For example, training manuals and publications of the government agency which employs workers in your field can be useful, particularly for technical and professional positions. A letter or visit to the government department involved may result in more specific study suggestions, and certainly will provide you with a more definite idea of the exact nature of the position you are seeking.

III. KINDS OF TESTS

Tests are used for purposes other than measuring knowledge and ability to perform specified duties. For some positions, it is equally important to test ability to make adjustments to new situations or to profit from training. In others, basic mental abilities not dependent on information are essential. Questions which test these things may not appear as pertinent to the duties of the position as those which test for knowledge and information. Yet they are often highly important parts of a fair examination. For very general questions, it is almost impossible to help you direct your study efforts. What we can do is to point out some of the more common of these general abilities needed in public service positions and describe some typical questions.

1) General information

Broad, general information has been found useful for predicting job success in some kinds of work. This is tested in a variety of ways, from vocabulary lists to questions about current events. Basic background in some field of work, such as sociology or economics, may be sampled in a group of questions. Often these are principles which have become familiar to most persons through exposure rather than through formal training. It is difficult to advise you how to study for these questions; being alert to the world around you is our best suggestion.

2) Verbal ability

An example of an ability needed in many positions is verbal or language ability. Verbal ability is, in brief, the ability to use and understand words. Vocabulary and grammar tests are typical measures of this ability. Reading comprehension or paragraph interpretation questions are common in many kinds of civil service tests. You are given a paragraph of written material and asked to find its central meaning.

3) Numerical ability

Number skills can be tested by the familiar arithmetic problem, by checking paired lists of numbers to see which are alike and which are different, or by interpreting charts and graphs. In the latter test, a graph may be printed in the test booklet which you are asked to use as the basis for answering questions.

4) Observation

A popular test for law-enforcement positions is the observation test. A picture is shown to you for several minutes, then taken away. Questions about the picture test your ability to observe both details and larger elements.

5) Following directions

In many positions in the public service, the employee must be able to carry out written instructions dependably and accurately. You may be given a chart with several columns, each column listing a variety of information. The questions require you to carry out directions involving the information given in the chart.

6) Skills and aptitudes

Performance tests effectively measure some manual skills and aptitudes. When the skill is one in which you are trained, such as typing or shorthand, you can practice. These tests are often very much like those given in business school or high school courses. For many of the other skills and aptitudes, however, no short-time preparation can be made. Skills and abilities natural to you or that you have developed throughout your lifetime are being tested.

Many of the general questions just described provide all the data needed to answer the questions and ask you to use your reasoning ability to find the answers. Your best preparation for these tests, as well as for tests of facts and ideas, is to be at your physical and mental best. You, no doubt, have your own methods of getting into an exam-taking mood and keeping "in shape." The next section lists some ideas on this subject.

IV. KINDS OF QUESTIONS

Only rarely is the "essay" question, which you answer in narrative form, used in civil service tests. Civil service tests are usually of the short-answer type. Full instructions for answering these questions will be given to you at the examination. But in case this is your first experience with short-answer questions and separate answer sheets, here is what you need to know:

1) Multiple-choice Questions

Most popular of the short-answer questions is the "multiple choice" or "best answer" question. It can be used, for example, to test for factual knowledge, ability to solve problems or judgment in meeting situations found at work.

A multiple-choice question is normally one of three types—

- It can begin with an incomplete statement followed by several possible endings. You are to find the one ending which *best* completes the statement, although some of the others may not be entirely wrong.
- It can also be a complete statement in the form of a question which is answered by choosing one of the statements listed.
- It can be in the form of a problem – again you select the best answer.

Here is an example of a multiple-choice question with a discussion which should give you some clues as to the method for choosing the right answer:

When an employee has a complaint about his assignment, the action which will *best* help him overcome his difficulty is to
   A. discuss his difficulty with his coworkers
   B. take the problem to the head of the organization
   C. take the problem to the person who gave him the assignment
   D. say nothing to anyone about his complaint

In answering this question, you should study each of the choices to find which is best. Consider choice "A" – Certainly an employee may discuss his complaint with fellow employees, but no change or improvement can result, and the complaint remains unresolved. Choice "B" is a poor choice since the head of the organization probably does not know what assignment you have been given, and taking your problem to him is known as "going over the head" of the supervisor. The supervisor, or person who made the assignment, is the person who can clarify it or correct any injustice. Choice "C" is, therefore, correct. To say nothing, as in choice "D," is unwise. Supervisors have and interest in knowing the problems employees are facing, and the employee is seeking a solution to his problem.

2) True/False Questions

The "true/false" or "right/wrong" form of question is sometimes used. Here a complete statement is given. Your job is to decide whether the statement is right or wrong.

SAMPLE: A roaming cell-phone call to a nearby city costs less than a non-roaming call to a distant city.

This statement is wrong, or false, since roaming calls are more expensive.
This is not a complete list of all possible question forms, although most of the others are variations of these common types. You will always get complete directions for

answering questions. Be sure you understand *how* to mark your answers – ask questions until you do.

V. RECORDING YOUR ANSWERS

Computer terminals are used more and more today for many different kinds of exams.

For an examination with very few applicants, you may be told to record your answers in the test booklet itself. Separate answer sheets are much more common. If this separate answer sheet is to be scored by machine – and this is often the case – it is highly important that you mark your answers correctly in order to get credit.

An electronic scoring machine is often used in civil service offices because of the speed with which papers can be scored. Machine-scored answer sheets must be marked with a pencil, which will be given to you. This pencil has a high graphite content which responds to the electronic scoring machine. As a matter of fact, stray dots may register as answers, so do not let your pencil rest on the answer sheet while you are pondering the correct answer. Also, if your pencil lead breaks or is otherwise defective, ask for another.

Since the answer sheet will be dropped in a slot in the scoring machine, be careful not to bend the corners or get the paper crumpled.

The answer sheet normally has five vertical columns of numbers, with 30 numbers to a column. These numbers correspond to the question numbers in your test booklet. After each number, going across the page are four or five pairs of dotted lines. These short dotted lines have small letters or numbers above them. The first two pairs may also have a "T" or "F" above the letters. This indicates that the first two pairs only are to be used if the questions are of the true-false type. If the questions are multiple choice, disregard the "T" and "F" and pay attention only to the small letters or numbers. Answer your questions in the manner of the sample that follows:

32. The largest city in the United States is
   A. Washington, D.C.
   B. New York City
   C. Chicago
   D. Detroit
   E. San Francisco

1) Choose the answer you think is best. (New York City is the largest, so "B" is correct.)
2) Find the row of dotted lines numbered the same as the question you are answering. (Find row number 32)
3) Find the pair of dotted lines corresponding to the answer. (Find the pair of lines under the mark "B.")
4) Make a solid black mark between the dotted lines.

VI. BEFORE THE TEST

Common sense will help you find procedures to follow to get ready for an examination. Too many of us, however, overlook these sensible measures. Indeed, nervousness and fatigue have been found to be the most serious reasons why applicants fail to do their best on civil service tests. Here is a list of reminders:

- Begin your preparation early – Don't wait until the last minute to go scurrying around for books and materials or to find out what the position is all about.
- Prepare continuously – An hour a night for a week is better than an all-night cram session. This has been definitely established. What is more, a night a week for a month will return better dividends than crowding your study into a shorter period of time.
- Locate the place of the exam – You have been sent a notice telling you when and where to report for the examination. If the location is in a different town or otherwise unfamiliar to you, it would be well to inquire the best route and learn something about the building.
- Relax the night before the test – Allow your mind to rest. Do not study at all that night. Plan some mild recreation or diversion; then go to bed early and get a good night's sleep.
- Get up early enough to make a leisurely trip to the place for the test – This way unforeseen events, traffic snarls, unfamiliar buildings, etc. will not upset you.
- Dress comfortably – A written test is not a fashion show. You will be known by number and not by name, so wear something comfortable.
- Leave excess paraphernalia at home – Shopping bags and odd bundles will get in your way. You need bring only the items mentioned in the official notice you received; usually everything you need is provided. Do not bring reference books to the exam. They will only confuse those last minutes and be taken away from you when in the test room.
- Arrive somewhat ahead of time – If because of transportation schedules you must get there very early, bring a newspaper or magazine to take your mind off yourself while waiting.
- Locate the examination room – When you have found the proper room, you will be directed to the seat or part of the room where you will sit. Sometimes you are given a sheet of instructions to read while you are waiting. Do not fill out any forms until you are told to do so; just read them and be prepared.
- Relax and prepare to listen to the instructions
- If you have any physical problem that may keep you from doing your best, be sure to tell the test administrator. If you are sick or in poor health, you really cannot do your best on the exam. You can come back and take the test some other time.

VII. AT THE TEST

The day of the test is here and you have the test booklet in your hand. The temptation to get going is very strong. Caution! There is more to success than knowing the right answers. You must know how to identify your papers and understand variations in the type of short-answer question used in this particular examination. Follow these suggestions for maximum results from your efforts:

1) Cooperate with the monitor

The test administrator has a duty to create a situation in which you can be as much at ease as possible. He will give instructions, tell you when to begin, check to see that you are marking your answer sheet correctly, and so on. He is not there to guard you, although he will see that your competitors do not take unfair advantage. He wants to help you do your best.

2) Listen to all instructions

Don't jump the gun! Wait until you understand all directions. In most civil service tests you get more time than you need to answer the questions. So don't be in a hurry. Read each word of instructions until you clearly understand the meaning. Study the examples, listen to all announcements and follow directions. Ask questions if you do not understand what to do.

3) Identify your papers

Civil service exams are usually identified by number only. You will be assigned a number; you must not put your name on your test papers. Be sure to copy your number correctly. Since more than one exam may be given, copy your exact examination title.

4) Plan your time

Unless you are told that a test is a "speed" or "rate of work" test, speed itself is usually not important. Time enough to answer all the questions will be provided, but this does not mean that you have all day. An overall time limit has been set. Divide the total time (in minutes) by the number of questions to determine the approximate time you have for each question.

5) Do not linger over difficult questions

If you come across a difficult question, mark it with a paper clip (useful to have along) and come back to it when you have been through the booklet. One caution if you do this – be sure to skip a number on your answer sheet as well. Check often to be sure that you have not lost your place and that you are marking in the row numbered the same as the question you are answering.

6) Read the questions

Be sure you know what the question asks! Many capable people are unsuccessful because they failed to *read* the questions correctly.

7) Answer all questions

Unless you have been instructed that a penalty will be deducted for incorrect answers, it is better to guess than to omit a question.

8) Speed tests

It is often better NOT to guess on speed tests. It has been found that on timed tests people are tempted to spend the last few seconds before time is called in marking answers at random – without even reading them – in the hope of picking up a few extra points. To discourage this practice, the instructions may warn you that your score will be "corrected" for guessing. That is, a penalty will be applied. The incorrect answers will be deducted from the correct ones, or some other penalty formula will be used.

9) Review your answers

If you finish before time is called, go back to the questions you guessed or omitted to give them further thought. Review other answers if you have time.

10) Return your test materials

If you are ready to leave before others have finished or time is called, take ALL your materials to the monitor and leave quietly. Never take any test material with you. The monitor can discover whose papers are not complete, and taking a test booklet may be grounds for disqualification.

VIII. EXAMINATION TECHNIQUES

1) Read the general instructions carefully. These are usually printed on the first page of the exam booklet. As a rule, these instructions refer to the timing of the examination; the fact that you should not start work until the signal and must stop work at a signal, etc. If there are any *special* instructions, such as a choice of questions to be answered, make sure that you note this instruction carefully.

2) When you are ready to start work on the examination, that is as soon as the signal has been given, read the instructions to each question booklet, underline any key words or phrases, such as *least, best, outline, describe* and the like. In this way you will tend to answer as requested rather than discover on reviewing your paper that you *listed without describing*, that you selected the *worst* choice rather than the *best* choice, etc.

3) If the examination is of the objective or multiple-choice type – that is, each question will also give a series of possible answers: A, B, C or D, and you are called upon to select the best answer and write the letter next to that answer on your answer paper – it is advisable to start answering each question in turn. There may be anywhere from 50 to 100 such questions in the three or four hours allotted and you can see how much time would be taken if you read through all the questions before beginning to answer any. Furthermore, if you come across a question or group of questions which you know would be difficult to answer, it would undoubtedly affect your handling of all the other questions.

4) If the examination is of the essay type and contains but a few questions, it is a moot point as to whether you should read all the questions before starting to answer any one. Of course, if you are given a choice – say five out of seven and the like – then it is essential to read all the questions so you can eliminate the two that are most difficult. If, however, you are asked to answer all the questions, there may be danger in trying to answer the easiest one first because you may find that you will spend too much time on it. The best technique is to answer the first question, then proceed to the second, etc.

5) Time your answers. Before the exam begins, write down the time it started, then add the time allowed for the examination and write down the time it must be completed, then divide the time available somewhat as follows:

- If 3-1/2 hours are allowed, that would be 210 minutes. If you have 80 objective-type questions, that would be an average of 2-1/2 minutes per question. Allow yourself no more than 2 minutes per question, or a total of 160 minutes, which will permit about 50 minutes to review.
- If for the time allotment of 210 minutes there are 7 essay questions to answer, that would average about 30 minutes a question. Give yourself only 25 minutes per question so that you have about 35 minutes to review.

6) The most important instruction is to *read each question* and make sure you know what is wanted. The second most important instruction is to *time yourself properly* so that you answer every question. The third most important instruction is to *answer every question*. Guess if you have to but include something for each question. Remember that you will receive no credit for a blank and will probably receive some credit if you write something in answer to an essay question. If you guess a letter – say "B" for a multiple-choice question – you may have guessed right. If you leave a blank as an answer to a multiple-choice question, the examiners may respect your feelings but it will not add a point to your score. Some exams may penalize you for wrong answers, so in such cases *only*, you may not want to guess unless you have some basis for your answer.

7) Suggestions
   a. Objective-type questions
      1. Examine the question booklet for proper sequence of pages and questions
      2. Read all instructions carefully
      3. Skip any question which seems too difficult; return to it after all other questions have been answered
      4. Apportion your time properly; do not spend too much time on any single question or group of questions
      5. Note and underline key words – *all, most, fewest, least, best, worst, same, opposite,* etc.
      6. Pay particular attention to negatives
      7. Note unusual option, e.g., unduly long, short, complex, different or similar in content to the body of the question
      8. Observe the use of "hedging" words – *probably, may, most likely,* etc.
      9. Make sure that your answer is put next to the same number as the question
      10. Do not second-guess unless you have good reason to believe the second answer is definitely more correct
      11. Cross out original answer if you decide another answer is more accurate; do not erase until you are ready to hand your paper in
      12. Answer all questions; guess unless instructed otherwise
      13. Leave time for review

   b. Essay questions
      1. Read each question carefully
      2. Determine exactly what is wanted. Underline key words or phrases.
      3. Decide on outline or paragraph answer

4. Include many different points and elements unless asked to develop any one or two points or elements
5. Show impartiality by giving pros and cons unless directed to select one side only
6. Make and write down any assumptions you find necessary to answer the questions
7. Watch your English, grammar, punctuation and choice of words
8. Time your answers; don't crowd material

8) Answering the essay question

Most essay questions can be answered by framing the specific response around several key words or ideas. Here are a few such key words or ideas:

M's: manpower, materials, methods, money, management
P's: purpose, program, policy, plan, procedure, practice, problems, pitfalls, personnel, public relations

   a. Six basic steps in handling problems:
     1. Preliminary plan and background development
     2. Collect information, data and facts
     3. Analyze and interpret information, data and facts
     4. Analyze and develop solutions as well as make recommendations
     5. Prepare report and sell recommendations
     6. Install recommendations and follow up effectiveness

   b. Pitfalls to avoid
     1. *Taking things for granted* – A statement of the situation does not necessarily imply that each of the elements is necessarily true; for example, a complaint may be invalid and biased so that all that can be taken for granted is that a complaint has been registered
     2. *Considering only one side of a situation* – Wherever possible, indicate several alternatives and then point out the reasons you selected the best one
     3. *Failing to indicate follow up* – Whenever your answer indicates action on your part, make certain that you will take proper follow-up action to see how successful your recommendations, procedures or actions turn out to be
     4. *Taking too long in answering any single question* – Remember to time your answers properly

IX. AFTER THE TEST

Scoring procedures differ in detail among civil service jurisdictions although the general principles are the same. Whether the papers are hand-scored or graded by machine we have described, they are nearly always graded by number. That is, the person who marks the paper knows only the number – never the name – of the applicant. Not until all the papers have been graded will they be matched with names. If other tests, such as training and experience or oral interview ratings have been given, scores will be combined. Different parts of the examination usually have different weights. For example, the written test might count 60 percent of the final grade, and a rating of training and experience 40 percent. In many jurisdictions, veterans will have a certain number of points added to their grades.

After the final grade has been determined, the names are placed in grade order and an eligible list is established. There are various methods for resolving ties between those who get the same final grade – probably the most common is to place first the name of the person whose application was received first. Job offers are made from the eligible list in the order the names appear on it. You will be notified of your grade and your rank as soon as all these computations have been made. This will be done as rapidly as possible.

People who are found to meet the requirements in the announcement are called "eligibles." Their names are put on a list of eligible candidates. An eligible's chances of getting a job depend on how high he stands on this list and how fast agencies are filling jobs from the list.

When a job is to be filled from a list of eligibles, the agency asks for the names of people on the list of eligibles for that job. When the civil service commission receives this request, it sends to the agency the names of the three people highest on this list. Or, if the job to be filled has specialized requirements, the office sends the agency the names of the top three persons who meet these requirements from the general list.

The appointing officer makes a choice from among the three people whose names were sent to him. If the selected person accepts the appointment, the names of the others are put back on the list to be considered for future openings.

That is the rule in hiring from all kinds of eligible lists, whether they are for typist, carpenter, chemist, or something else. For every vacancy, the appointing officer has his choice of any one of the top three eligibles on the list. This explains why the person whose name is on top of the list sometimes does not get an appointment when some of the persons lower on the list do. If the appointing officer chooses the second or third eligible, the No. 1 eligible does not get a job at once, but stays on the list until he is appointed or the list is terminated.

X. HOW TO PASS THE INTERVIEW TEST

The examination for which you applied requires an oral interview test. You have already taken the written test and you are now being called for the interview test – the final part of the formal examination.

You may think that it is not possible to prepare for an interview test and that there are no procedures to follow during an interview. Our purpose is to point out some things you can do in advance that will help you and some good rules to follow and pitfalls to avoid while you are being interviewed.

What is an interview supposed to test?

The written examination is designed to test the technical knowledge and competence of the candidate; the oral is designed to evaluate intangible qualities, not readily measured otherwise, and to establish a list showing the relative fitness of each candidate – as measured against his competitors – for the position sought. Scoring is not on the basis of "right" and "wrong," but on a sliding scale of values ranging from "not passable" to "outstanding." As a matter of fact, it is possible to achieve a relatively low score without a single "incorrect" answer because of evident weakness in the qualities being measured.

Occasionally, an examination may consist entirely of an oral test – either an individual or a group oral. In such cases, information is sought concerning the technical knowledges and abilities of the candidate, since there has been no written examination for this purpose. More commonly, however, an oral test is used to supplement a written examination.

Who conducts interviews?

The composition of oral boards varies among different jurisdictions. In nearly all, a representative of the personnel department serves as chairman. One of the members of the board may be a representative of the department in which the candidate would work. In some cases, "outside experts" are used, and, frequently, a businessman or some other representative of the general public is asked to serve. Labor and management or other special groups may be represented. The aim is to secure the services of experts in the appropriate field.

However the board is composed, it is a good idea (and not at all improper or unethical) to ascertain in advance of the interview who the members are and what groups they represent. When you are introduced to them, you will have some idea of their backgrounds and interests, and at least you will not stutter and stammer over their names.

What should be done before the interview?

While knowledge about the board members is useful and takes some of the surprise element out of the interview, there is other preparation which is more substantive. It *is* possible to prepare for an oral interview – in several ways:

1) Keep a copy of your application and review it carefully before the interview

This may be the only document before the oral board, and the starting point of the interview. Know what education and experience you have listed there, and the sequence and dates of all of it. Sometimes the board will ask you to review the highlights of your experience for them; you should not have to hem and haw doing it.

2) Study the class specification and the examination announcement

Usually, the oral board has one or both of these to guide them. The qualities, characteristics or knowledges required by the position sought are stated in these documents. They offer valuable clues as to the nature of the oral interview. For example, if the job involves supervisory responsibilities, the announcement will usually indicate that knowledge of modern supervisory methods and the qualifications of the candidate as a supervisor will be tested. If so, you can expect such questions, frequently in the form of a hypothetical situation which you are expected to solve. NEVER go into an oral without knowledge of the duties and responsibilities of the job you seek.

3) Think through each qualification required

Try to visualize the kind of questions you would ask if you were a board member. How well could you answer them? Try especially to appraise your own knowledge and background in each area, *measured against the job sought*, and identify any areas in which you are weak. Be critical and realistic – do not flatter yourself.

4) Do some general reading in areas in which you feel you may be weak

For example, if the job involves supervision and your past experience has NOT, some general reading in supervisory methods and practices, particularly in the field of human relations, might be useful. Do NOT study agency procedures or detailed manuals. The oral board will be testing your understanding and capacity, not your memory.

5) Get a good night's sleep and watch your general health and mental attitude

You will want a clear head at the interview. Take care of a cold or any other minor ailment, and of course, no hangovers.

What should be done on the day of the interview?

Now comes the day of the interview itself. Give yourself plenty of time to get there. Plan to arrive somewhat ahead of the scheduled time, particularly if your appointment is in the fore part of the day. If a previous candidate fails to appear, the board might be ready for you a bit early. By early afternoon an oral board is almost invariably behind schedule if there are many candidates, and you may have to wait. Take along a book or magazine to read, or your application to review, but leave any extraneous material in the waiting room when you go in for your interview. In any event, relax and compose yourself.

The matter of dress is important. The board is forming impressions about you – from your experience, your manners, your attitude, and your appearance. Give your personal appearance careful attention. Dress your best, but not your flashiest. Choose conservative, appropriate clothing, and be sure it is immaculate. This is a business interview, and your appearance should indicate that you regard it as such. Besides, being well groomed and properly dressed will help boost your confidence.

Sooner or later, someone will call your name and escort you into the interview room. *This is it.* From here on you are on your own. It is too late for any more preparation. But remember, you asked for this opportunity to prove your fitness, and you are here because your request was granted.

What happens when you go in?

The usual sequence of events will be as follows: The clerk (who is often the board stenographer) will introduce you to the chairman of the oral board, who will introduce you to the other members of the board. Acknowledge the introductions before you sit down. Do not be surprised if you find a microphone facing you or a stenotypist sitting by. Oral interviews are usually recorded in the event of an appeal or other review.

Usually the chairman of the board will open the interview by reviewing the highlights of your education and work experience from your application – primarily for the benefit of the other members of the board, as well as to get the material into the record. Do not interrupt or comment unless there is an error or significant misinterpretation; if that is the case, do not hesitate. But do not quibble about insignificant matters. Also, he will usually ask you some question about your education, experience or your present job – partly to get you to start talking and to establish the interviewing "rapport." He may start the actual questioning, or turn it over to one of the other members. Frequently, each member undertakes the questioning on a particular area, one in which he is perhaps most competent, so you can expect each member to participate in the examination. Because time is limited, you may also expect some rather abrupt switches in the direction the questioning takes, so do not be upset by it. Normally, a board member will not pursue a single line of questioning unless he discovers a particular strength or weakness.

After each member has participated, the chairman will usually ask whether any member has any further questions, then will ask you if you have anything you wish to add. Unless you are expecting this question, it may floor you. Worse, it may start you off on an extended, extemporaneous speech. The board is not usually seeking more information. The question is principally to offer you a last opportunity to present further qualifications or to indicate that you have nothing to add. So, if you feel that a significant qualification or characteristic has been overlooked, it is proper to point it out in a sentence or so. Do not compliment the board on the thoroughness of their examination – they have been sketchy, and you know it. If you wish, merely say, "No thank you, I have nothing further to add." This is a point where you can "talk yourself out" of a good impression or fail to present an important bit of information. Remember, *you close the interview yourself.*

The chairman will then say, "That is all, Mr. _____, thank you." Do not be startled; the interview is over, and quicker than you think. Thank him, gather your belongings and take your leave. Save your sigh of relief for the other side of the door.

How to put your best foot forward

Throughout this entire process, you may feel that the board individually and collectively is trying to pierce your defenses, seek out your hidden weaknesses and embarrass and confuse you. Actually, this is not true. They are obliged to make an appraisal of your qualifications for the job you are seeking, and they want to see you in your best light. Remember, they must interview all candidates and a non-cooperative candidate may become a failure in spite of their best efforts to bring out his qualifications. Here are 15 suggestions that will help you:

1) Be natural – Keep your attitude confident, not cocky

If you are not confident that you can do the job, do not expect the board to be. Do not apologize for your weaknesses, try to bring out your strong points. The board is interested in a positive, not negative, presentation. Cockiness will antagonize any board member and make him wonder if you are covering up a weakness by a false show of strength.

2) Get comfortable, but don't lounge or sprawl

Sit erectly but not stiffly. A careless posture may lead the board to conclude that you are careless in other things, or at least that you are not impressed by the importance of the occasion. Either conclusion is natural, even if incorrect. Do not fuss with your clothing, a pencil or an ashtray. Your hands may occasionally be useful to emphasize a point; do not let them become a point of distraction.

3) Do not wisecrack or make small talk

This is a serious situation, and your attitude should show that you consider it as such. Further, the time of the board is limited – they do not want to waste it, and neither should you.

4) Do not exaggerate your experience or abilities

In the first place, from information in the application or other interviews and sources, the board may know more about you than you think. Secondly, you probably will not get away with it. An experienced board is rather adept at spotting such a situation, so do not take the chance.

5) If you know a board member, do not make a point of it, yet do not hide it

Certainly you are not fooling him, and probably not the other members of the board. Do not try to take advantage of your acquaintanceship – it will probably do you little good.

6) Do not dominate the interview

Let the board do that. They will give you the clues – do not assume that you have to do all the talking. Realize that the board has a number of questions to ask you, and do not try to take up all the interview time by showing off your extensive knowledge of the answer to the first one.

7) Be attentive

You only have 20 minutes or so, and you should keep your attention at its sharpest throughout. When a member is addressing a problem or question to you, give him your undivided attention. Address your reply principally to him, but do not exclude the other board members.

8) Do not interrupt

A board member may be stating a problem for you to analyze. He will ask you a question when the time comes. Let him state the problem, and wait for the question.

9) Make sure you understand the question

Do not try to answer until you are sure what the question is. If it is not clear, restate it in your own words or ask the board member to clarify it for you. However, do not haggle about minor elements.

10) Reply promptly but not hastily

A common entry on oral board rating sheets is "candidate responded readily," or "candidate hesitated in replies." Respond as promptly and quickly as you can, but do not jump to a hasty, ill-considered answer.

11) Do not be peremptory in your answers

A brief answer is proper – but do not fire your answer back. That is a losing game from your point of view. The board member can probably ask questions much faster than you can answer them.

12) Do not try to create the answer you think the board member wants

He is interested in what kind of mind you have and how it works – not in playing games. Furthermore, he can usually spot this practice and will actually grade you down on it.

13) Do not switch sides in your reply merely to agree with a board member

Frequently, a member will take a contrary position merely to draw you out and to see if you are willing and able to defend your point of view. Do not start a debate, yet do not surrender a good position. If a position is worth taking, it is worth defending.

14) Do not be afraid to admit an error in judgment if you are shown to be wrong

The board knows that you are forced to reply without any opportunity for careful consideration. Your answer may be demonstrably wrong. If so, admit it and get on with the interview.

15) Do not dwell at length on your present job

The opening question may relate to your present assignment. Answer the question but do not go into an extended discussion. You are being examined for a *new* job, not your present one. As a matter of fact, try to phrase ALL your answers in terms of the job for which you are being examined.

Basis of Rating

Probably you will forget most of these "do's" and "don'ts" when you walk into the oral interview room. Even remembering them all will not ensure you a passing grade. Perhaps you did not have the qualifications in the first place. But remembering them will help you to put your best foot forward, without treading on the toes of the board members.

Rumor and popular opinion to the contrary notwithstanding, an oral board wants you to make the best appearance possible. They know you are under pressure – but they also want to see how you respond to it as a guide to what your reaction would be under the pressures of the job you seek. They will be influenced by the degree of poise you display, the personal traits you show and the manner in which you respond.

ABOUT THIS BOOK

This book contains tests divided into Examination Sections. Go through each test, answering every question in the margin. At the end of each test look at the answer key and check your answers. On the ones you got wrong, look at the right answer choice and learn. Do not fill in the answers first. Do not memorize the questions and answers, but understand the answer and principles involved. On your test, the questions will likely be different from the samples. Questions are changed and new ones added. If you understand these past questions you should have success with any changes that arise. Tests may consist of several types of questions. We have additional books on each subject should more study be advisable or necessary for you. Finally, the more you study, the better prepared you will be. This book is intended to be the last thing you study before you walk into the examination room. Prior study of relevant texts is also recommended. NLC publishes some of these in our Fundamental Series. Knowledge and good sense are important factors in passing your exam. Good luck also helps. So now study this Passbook, absorb the material contained within and take that knowledge into the examination. Then do your best to pass that exam.

EXAMINATION SECTION

EXAMINATION SECTION
TEST I

DIRECTIONS: Each question or incomplete statement is followed by several suggested answers or completions. Select the one that BEST answers the question or completes the statement. *PRINT THE LETTER OF THE CORRECT ANSWER IN THE SPACE AT THE RIGHT.*

1. The KEY figure in any custodial safety program is the
   A. custodian   B. cleaner   C. mayor   D. commissioner

1._____

2. A custodian must inspect or have a maintenance man inspect every window cleaner's safety belt AT LEAST
   A. each time the windows are washed
   B. once a month
   C. once a year
   D. once every second year

2._____

3. A custodian's written instruction to his staff on the subject of security in public buildings should include instructions to
   A. exclude the public at all times
   B. admit the public at all times
   C. admit the public only if they are neat and well-dressed
   D. admit the public during specified hours

3._____

4. A custodian in charge of a building who is normally on duty during the daytime hours in a building which is cleaned at night should
   A. never make night inspections since he is not responsible for the cleanliness of the building
   B. make night inspections at least once a year
   C. never make night inspections because the cleaners will think he is spying on them
   D. make night inspections at least twice a month

4._____

5. The employee MOST likely to find the nests and runways a building is a of roaches and vermin in
   A. maintenance man
   C. building custodian
   B. night cleaner
   D. stationary fireman

5._____

6. When mopping, the pails containing the cleaning solutions should be
   A. slid along the floor to avoid injury due to lifting
   B. kept off the floor preferably on a rolling platform
   C. shifted from place to place using the mop
   D. equipped with a spigot for applying the mopping solution

6._____

7. Of the following, the item that is considered a concrete floor sealer is
   A. water wax   B. sodium hypochlorite
   C. sodium silicate   D. linseed oil

7._____

8. A material COMMONLY used in detergents is
    A. rock salt   B. Glauber's salt
    C. tri-sodium phosphate   D. monosodium glutamate

8._____

9. A disinfectant material is one that will
    A. kill germs
    B. dissolve soil and stop odors
    C. give a clean odor and cover a disagreeable odor
    D. prevent soil buildup

9._____

10. When scrubbing a wooden floor, it is ADVISABLE to
    A. flood the surface with the cleaning solution in order to float the soil out of all crevices
    B. hose off the loosened soil before starting the scrubbing operation
    C. pick up the used solution as soon as possible
    D. mix a mild acid with the cleaning solution in order to clean the surface quickly

10._____

11. Before starting a wall washing operation, it is BEST to
    A. check the temperature of the water
    B. soak the sponge to be used
    C. check the pH of the mixed cleaning solution
    D. dust the wall to be washed

11._____

12. Of the following, the MOST nearly correct statement regarding the economical operation of the heating system in a building is that
    A. the heat should always be shut down at 4 P.M. and turned on at 8 A.M.
    B. the heat should be shut down only over the weekend
    C. it is best to keep the heat on at all times so that the number of complaints are kept to a minimum
    D. the times at which the heat is shut down and turned on should be varied depending on the prevailing outdoor temperature

12._____

13. A floor made of marble or granite chips imbedded in cement is USUALLY called
    A. terrazzo   B. linoleum   C. palmetto   D. parquet

13._____

14. In a 4-wire, 3-phase electrical supply system, the voltage between one phase and ground used for the lighting load is MOST NEARLY
    A. 440   B. 230   C. 208   D. 115

14._____

15. Of the following, the one that takes the place of a fuse in an electrical circuit is a
    A. transformer   B. circuit breaker
    C. condenser   D. knife switch

15._____

16. Gas bills are USUALLY computed on the basis of
    A. cubic feet   B. gallons   C. pounds   D. kilowatts

16._____

17. An operating oil-fired steam boiler explosion may some- times be caused by   17._____
    A. carrying too high a water level in the boiler
    B. inadequate purging of combustion chamber between fires
    C. overfiring the boiler
    D. carrying too nigh an oil temperature

18. The one of the following commercial sizes of anthracite which is the LARGEST in size is   18._____
    A. stove   B. chestnut   C. pea   D. rice

19. Assume that six windows of a public building facing one street have been consistently   19._____
broken by boys playing ball after hours and over weekends.
The BEST solution to this problem is to
    A. post a no ball playing sign on the wall
    B. erect protective screening outside the six windows
    C. post a guard on weekend patrol duty
    D. request special weekend police protection for the property
    E.

20. The BEST method or tool to use for cleaning dust from an unplastered cinderblock   20._____
wall is   .
    A. a tampico brush with stock cleaning solution
    B. a vacuum cleaner
    C. water under pressure from hose and nozzle
    D. a feather duster

21. Of the following, the LARGEST individual item of expense LARGEST individual item   21._____
of expense in operating a public building is generally the cost of
    A. cleaning   B. heating fuel
    B. electricity   D. elevator service

22. The CHIEF purpose for changing the handle of a floor brush from one side of the   22._____
brush block to the other side is to
    A. allow the janitor to change hands
    B. make both sides of the brush equally dirty
    C. give both sides of the brush equal wear
    D. change the angle of sweeping

23. Of the following, the weight of mop MOST likely used in the nightly mopping of   23._____
corridors, halls, or lobbies is ounce.
    A. 8   B. 16   C. 24   D. 50

24. After a sweeping assignment is completed, floor brushes should be stored   24._____
    A. in a pan of water
    B. by hanging the brushes on pegs or nails
    C. by piling the brushes on each other carefully
    D. in a normal sweeping position, bristles resting on the floor

25. Nylon treated scrubbing discs   25._____
    A. require more water than scrubbing brushes
    B. require more detergent solution than scrubbing brushes
    C. must be used with cold water only
    D. are generally more effective than steel wool pads

26. Of the following, the BEST material to use to clean exterior bronze is
    A. pumice
    B. paste wax
    C. wire wheel on portable buffer
    D. lemon oil polish

26._____

27. The use of trisodium phosphate in cleaning polished marble should be AVOIDED because it
    A. may cause spalling
    B. discolors the surface of the marble
    C. builds up a slick surface on the marble
    D. pits the glazed surface and bleaches the marble

27._____

28. The floor area, in square feet, on which a properly treated dustless sweeping cloth can be used before the cloth must be washed is
    A. 500 - 1000
    B. 2000 - 3000
    C. 4000 - 6000
    D. 8000 - 10000

28._____

29. A cleaning woman working a six-hour shift should be able to cover (clean)_____ Gilbert work units.
    A. 100-200
    B. 400-500
    C. 1100-1200
    D. 6000-7000

29._____

30. An incipient fire is one which
    A. has just started and can be readily extinguished using an ordinary hand extinguisher
    B. occurs only in motor vehicles
    C. is burning out of control in a storeroom
    D. is a banked coal fire

30._____

31. Maintaining room temperature at 75°F in the winter time will increase fuel consumption above the amount needed to maintain 70°F by APPROXIMATELY
    A. 5%
    B. 10%
    C. 15%
    D. 20%

31._____

32. Of the following, the one which represents the BEST practical combustion condition in an oil-fired low pressure steam plant is_____stack temperature.
    A. 8% CO_2 - 500°F
    B. 13% CO_2 - 400°F
    C. 10% CO_2 - 700°F
    D. 6% CO_2 - 400°F

32._____

33. An office has floor dimensions of 16ft. 6 in. wide by 22 ft. 0 in. long. The floor area of this office, in square feet, is MOST NEARLY
    A. 143
    B. 263
    C. 363
    D. 463

33._____

34. Dollies are USUALLY used
    A. as convenient platforms upon which to store items
    B. as ornamental protective covers
    C. to raise items to the required level
    D. to transport items from one place to another

34._____

35. When lifting a heavy object from a table, which of the following rules is it MOST important to observe?

    A. Do not bend your knees.
    B. Do not stand too close to the object
    C. Keep your back straight.
    D. Keep your shoulder level with the object.

35._____

36. The FIRST objective of all fire prevention is
    A. confining fire to a limited area
    B. safeguarding life against fire
    C. reducing insurance rates
    D. preventing property damage
    E.

36._____

37. A custodian should know the equipment used in his work well enough to
    A. make any repairs which might be needed
    B. know what parts to remove in case of breakdown
    C. anticipate any reasonable possibility of a breakdown
    D. know all the lubricants specified by the manufacturer

37._____

38. The PRIMARY responsibility of a supervising custodian is to
    A. make friends of all subordinates
    B. search for new methods of doing the work
    C. win the respect of his superior
    D. get the work done properly within a reasonable time

38._____

39. When a custodian believes that the work of a subordinate is below standard, he should
    A. assign the employee to work that is considered undesirable
    B. do nothing immediately in the hope that the employee will bring his work up to standard without any help from the supervisor
    C. reduce the privileges of the employee at once
    D. discuss it as soon as possible with the employee

39._____

40. An office worker frequently complains to the custodian that her office is poorly illuminated.
    The BEST action for the custodian to follow is to
    A. ignore the complaints as those of an habitual crank
    B. inform the worker that illumination is a fixed item built into the building originally and evidently is the result of faulty planning by the architect
    C. request a licensed electrician to install additional ceiling lights
    D. investigate for faulty illumination features in the room, such as dirty lamp globes and incorrect lamp wattages

40._____

_____

KEY (CORRECT ANSWERS)

1.	A	11.	D	21.	A	31.	D
2.	C	12.	D	22.	C	32.	B
3.	D	13.	A	23.	C	33.	C
4.	D	14.	D	24.	B	34.	D
5.	B	15.	B	25.	D	35.	C
6.	B	16.	A	26.	D	36.	B
7.	C	17.	B	27.	A	37.	C
8.	C	18.	A	28.	C	38.	D
9.	A	19.	B	29.	C	39.	D
10.	C	20.	B	30.	A	40.	D

_____

TEST 2

DIRECTIONS: Each question or incomplete statement is followed by several suggested answers or completions. Select the one that BEST answers the question or completes the statement. *PRINT THE LETTER OF THE CORRECT ANSWER IN THE SPACE AT THE RIGHT.*

1. Of the following, the MOST important reason for the custodian to plan work schedules for men under his supervision is that
   A. emergency situations can easily be handled if they should arise
   B. it insures that essential operations will be adequately covered
   C. the men will be more satisfied if a routine is established
   D. the relationship between the supervisor and his subordinate will be clarified

   1._____

2. Sealers for open-grained wood floors should NOT contain linseed oil because
   A. the linseed oil would damage the wood fibers
   B. the linseed oil would deteriorate mop strands
   C. water wax would penetrate the linseed oil sealer and rot the wood
   D. linseed oil on wood takes too long to dry satisfactorily before a floor finish could be applied

   2._____

3. When washing painted wall areas by hand, a man should be expected to wash each our an area, in square feet, equal to
   A. 75-125   B. 150-300   C. 400-600   D. 750-1000

   3._____

4. Of the following, the one that is MOST desirable to use in dusting furniture is a
   A. feather duster   B. paper towel
   C. counter brush   D. soft cotton cloth

   4._____

5. The one of the following floor types on which oily sweeping compound may be used is
   A. vinyl tile   B. concrete   C. linoleum   D. terrazzo

   5._____

6. A steam heating system where the steam and condensate flow in the same pipe is called a_____system.
   A. one pipe gravity return   B. sub-atmospheric
   C. vacuum return   D. zone control

   6._____

7. A test of a boiler by applying pressure equal to or greater than the maximum working pressure is called a test.

   A. hydrostatic   B. barometric
   C. hygroscopic   D. gyroscopic

   7._____

8. A stack switch as used with an oil burner
   A. shuts down the burner in case of non-ignition
   B. shuts down the burner in case of high stack temperatures
   C. controls the flow of secondary air
   D. operates the barometric damper

   8._____

9. The vertical pipes leading from the steam mains to the radiators are called
   A. drip lines   B. risers
   C. radiant coils   D. expansion joints

   9._____

10. Fuel oil storage tanks are equipped with vents. The purpose of these vents is to 10.____
   A. make tank soundings   B. check oil flash points
   C. fill the fuel tanks   D. allow air to mix

11. A compound gauge in a boiler room 11.____
   A. measures steam and water pressure
   B. shows the quantity of boiler treatment compound on hand
   C. measures pressures above and below atmospheric pressure
   D. indicates the degree of compounding in a steam engine
   E.

12. Of the following, the CHIEF purpose of insulating steam lines is to 12.____
   A. prevent loss of heat
   B. protect people from being burned by them
   C. prevent leaks
   D. protect the pipes against corrosion

13. The MOST important function of thermostatic traps on radiators is to 13.____
   A. regulate the heat given off by the radiator
   B. remove water and air from the radiator
   C. assist the steam pressure in filling the radiator
   D. maintain a vacuum within the radiator

14. The designation *1/8 - 27 N.P.T.* USUALLY indicates 14.____
   A. machine screw thread   B. pipe thread
   C. spur gear size   D. sprocket chain size

15. The size of a chisel is determined by its 15.____
   A. length   B. width   C. pitch   D. height

16. The cause of paint blisters is USUALLY 16.____
   A. moisture under the paint coat
   B. too thick a coat of paint
   C. tod much oil in paint
   D. the plaster pores not sealed properly

17. A wood-framed picture is to be attached to a plaster and hollow tile wall. 17.____
   Of the following, the proper installation would include the use of
   A. wire cut nails
   B. miracle glue
   C. expansion shields and screws
   D. self-tapping screws

18. The PROPER tool or method to use for driving a finish nail to the depth necessary 18.____
   for puttying when installing wood trim is
   A. countersink
   B. another nail of the same diameter
   C. a nail set
   D. a center punch

7

19. Faucet leakage in a large building is BEST controlled by periodic
    A. faucet replacement
    B. addition of a sealing compound to the water supply
    C. packing replacement
    D. faucet inspection and repair

19._____

20. Escutcheons are USUALLY located
    A. on kitchen cabinet drawers
    B. on windows
    C. around pipes, to cover pipe sleeve openings
    D. around armored electric cable going into a gem box

20._____

21. It is ADVISABLE to remove broken bulbs from light sockets with
    A. a wooden or hard rubber wedge
    B. pliers
    C. a hammer and chisel
    D. a fuse puller

21._____

22. A room 20' x 25' in area with a ceiling height of 9'6" is to be painted. One gallon of paint will cover 400 square feet.
The MINIMUM number of gallons necessary to give the four walls and the ceiling one coat of paint is
    A. 2   B. 3   C. 4   D. 5

22._____

23. Of the following, the ones on which gaskets are MOST likely to be used are
    A. threaded pipe plugs
    B. cast iron pipe nipples
    C. flanged pipe fittings
    D. threaded cast iron reducing tees

23._____

24. If a 110 volt lamp were used on a 220 volt circuit, the
    A. fuse would burn out   B. lamp would burn out
    B. line would overheat   D. lamp would flicker

24._____

25. The third prong on the plug of portable electric power tools of recent manufacture is for
    A. using the tool on a 3-phase power outlet
    B. eliminating interference in radio or television sets
    C. grounding the tool as a safety precaution
    D. using the tool on direct current circuits

25._____

26. When changing brushes on a scrubbing machine, of the following, the FIRST step to take is to
    A. lock the switch in the off position
    B. be sure the power cable electric plug supplying the machine is disconnected from the wall outlet
    C. place the machine on top of the positioned brushes
    D. dip the brushes in water

26._____

27. In cleaning away branches that have been broken off as a result of a severe storm,   27._____
one of your men comes in contact with a live electric line and falls unconscious.
After having removed him from contact, the FIRST thing to be done is to
    A. send for an inhalator to revive him
    B. administer mouth-to-mouth resuscitation
    C. search for the switch to prevent any other such cases
    D. loosen his clothing and begin rubbing his forehead to restore circulation

28. Of the following, the MOST effective way to reduce waste in cleaning equipment   28._____
and tools is by
    A. requiring a worn brush or broom to be returned before issuing a new one
    B. requiring the cleaners to use all cleaning tools for specific periods of time
    C. keeping careful records of how frequently cleaning equipment and tools are
       issued to cleaners
    D. making sure that cleaners use the tools properly

29. A window cleaner should carefully examine his safety belt   29._____
    A. once a week
    B. before he puts it on each time
    C. once a month
    D. once before he enters a building

30. One of your cleaners was injured as a result of slipping on an oily floor.   30._____
This type of accident is MOST likely due to
    A. defective equipment
    B. the physical condition of the cleaner
    C. failure to use proper safety appliances
    D. poor housekeeping

31. One important use of accident reports is to provide information that may be used   31._____
to reduce the possibility of similar accidents.
The MOST valuable entry on the report for this purpose is the
    A. name of the victim
    B. injury sustained by the victim
    C. cause of the accident
    D. location of the accident

32. Fires in buildings are of such complexity that   32._____
    A. no plans or methods of attack can be formulated in advance
    B. no planned procedures can be relied on
    C. an appointed committee is necessary to direct fighting at the fire
    D. the problem must be considered in advance and methods of attack formulated

33. Of the following types of fires, a soda-acid fire extinguisher is NOT   33._____
recommended for
    A. electric motor controls   B. waste paper
    C. waste rags   D. wood desks

33. Of the following types of fires, a soda-acid fire extinguisher is NOT recommended for
    B. electric motor controls   B. waste paper
    C. waste rags   D. wood desks

33._____

34. A foam-type fire extinguisher extinguishes fires by
    A. cooling only   B. drenching only
    C. smothering only   D. cooling and smothering

34._____

35. If a keg of nails had on it the words *Net Weight 10 pounds*, it would mean that the
    A. keg weighed 10 pounds without the nails
    B. nails and the keg together weighed 10 pounds
    C. nails weighed 10 pounds without the keg
    D. weight of 10 pounds is approximate

35._____

36. In deciding which items should be stored together, the one of the following factors which is usually of LEAST importance is
    A. activity   B. class   C. cost   D. size

36._____

37. Of the following, the MOST effective way to teach a subordinate how to store an item is to
    A. do it yourself while explaining
    B. explain the procedure verbally
    C. have him do it while you criticize
    D. let him look at photographs of the operation

37._____

38. If a cleaner is doing excellent work, then the PROPER action of the custodian is to
    A. give him preferential assignments as a reward
    B. tell the other cleaners what excellent work he is doing
    C. praise his work at the earliest opportunity
    D. do nothing since the man may become over-confident

38._____

39. A cleaner does very good work, but he has trouble getting to work on time. To get the man to come on time, you should
    A. bring him up on charges to stop the lateness once and for all
    B. have him report directly to you every time he is late
    C. talk over the problem with him to find its cause and possible solution
    D. threaten to transfer him if he cannot get to work on time

39._____

40. When the National flag is to be flown at half staff, it should ALWAYS be hoisted
    A. slowly to half staff
    B. slowly to the peak of staff and then lowered slowly to half staff
    C. briskly to the peak of staff and then lowered slowly to half staff
    D. briskly to the peak of staff and then lowered briskly to half staff

40._____

_____

10

KEY (CORRECT ANSWERS)

1.	B	11.	C	21.	A	31.	C
2.	D	12.	A	22.	C	32.	D
3.	B	13.	B	23.	C	33.	A
4.	D	14.	B	24.	B	34.	D
5.	B	15.	B	25.	C	35.	C
6.	A	16.	A	26.	B	36.	C
7.	A	17.	C	27.	B	37.	A
8.	A	18.	C	28.	D	38.	C
9.	B	19.	C	29.	B	39.	C
10.	D	20.	D	30.	D	40.	C

———

EXAMINATION SECTION
TEST 1

DIRECTION: Each question or Incomplete statement is followed by several suggested answers or completions. Select the one that BEST answers the question or completes the statement. *PRINT THE LETTER OF THE CORRECT ANSWER IN THE SPACE AT THE RIGHT.*

Questions 1-5.

DIRECTIONS: Column I lists cleaning jobs. Column II lists cleansing agents and devices. Select the PROPER cleansing agent from column II for each job in column I. Place the letter of the cleansing agent select in the space at the right corresponding to the number of the cleaning job.

COLUMN I	COLUMN II	
1. Chewing gum	A. Muriatic acid	1.____
2. Ink stains	B. Broad bladed knife	2.____
3. Fingermarks on glass	C. Kerosene	3.____
4. Rust stains on porcelain	D. Oxalic acid	4.____
5. Hardened dirt on porcelain	E. Lye	5.____
	F. Linseed oil	

6.   When the bristles of a floor brush have worn short. the brush should be   6.____

    A.   thrown away and the handles saved
    B.   saved and the brush used on rough cement floors
    C.   saved and used for high dusting in classrooms
    D.   saved and used for the weekly scrubbing of linoleum floors

7.   Feather dusters should NOT be used because they   7.____

    A.   take more time to use than other dusters
    B.   cannot be cleaned
    C.   do not take up the dust but merely move it from one place to another
    D.   do not stir up the dust and streak the furniture with dust rails

8.   Floors that are usually NOT waxed are those made of   8.____

    A.   pine wood   B.   mastic tile
    C.   rubber tile   D.   terrazzo

9.   For sweeping under radiators and other inaccessible places, the MOST appropriate tool   9.____
is the

    A.   counter brush   B.   dry mop
    C.   feather duster   D.   16" floor brush

10.   A cleansing agent that should NOT be used in the cleaning of windows is   10.____

A. water containing fine pumice
B. water containing a small amount of ammonia
C. water containing a little kerosene
D. a paste cleanser made from water and cleaning powder

11. The BEST way to dust desks is to use a 11.____

A. circular motion with soft dry cloth that has been washed
B. damp cloth, taking care not to disturb papers on the desk
C. soft cloth, moistened with oil, using a back and forth motion
D. back and forth motion with a soft dry cloth

12. Trisodium phosphate is a substance BEST used In 12.____

A. washing kalsomined walls
B. polishing of brass
C. washing mastic tile floors
D. clearing stoppages

13. Treated linoleum is PROPERLY cleaned by daily 13.____

A. dusting with a treated mop
B. sweeping with a floor brush
C. mopping with a weak soap solution
D. mopping after removal of dust with a floor brush

14. Of the following, the MOST proper use for chamois skin is 14.____

A. drying of window glass after washing
B. washing of window glass
C. polishing of metal fixtures
D. drying toilet bowls after washing

15. A squeegee is a tool which is used in 15.____

A. clearing stoppages in waste lines
B. the central vacuum cleaning system
C. cleaning inside boiler surfaces
D. drying windows after washing

16. Concrete and cement floors are usually painted a battleship gray color. 16.____
The MOST important reason for painting the floor is

A. to improve the appearance of the floor
B. the paint prevents the absorption of too much water when the floor is mopped
C. the paint makes the floor safer and less slippery
D. the concrete becomes harder and will not settle

17. A resin-base floor finish USUALLY 17.____

A. gives the highest lustre of all floor finishes
B. should be applied in one heavy coat
C. provides a slip-resistant surface
D. should not be used on asphalt tile

18. The one of the following cleaning operations on soft floors that generally requires MOST   18.____
NEARLY the same amount of time per 1,000 square feet as damp mopping is

    A. applying a thin coat of wax
    B. sweeping
    C. dust mopping
    D. wet mopping

19. Of the following cleaning jobs, the one that should be allowed the MOST time to com-   19.____
plete a 1,000 square foot area is

    A. vacuuming carpets
    B. washing painted walls
    C. stripping and waxing soft floors
    D. machine-scrubbing hard floors

20. When instructing your staff in the use of sodium silicate, you should tell them that it is   20.____
MOST commonly used to

    A. seal concrete floors   B. condition leather
    C. treat boiler water   D. neutralize acid wastes

21. Cleaners should be instructed that dust mopping is LEAST appropriate for removing light   21.____
soil from _____ floors.

    A. terrazzo   B. unsealed concrete
    C. resin-finished soft   D. sealed wood

22. Of the following, the substance that should be recommended for polishing hardwood fur-   22.____
niture is

    A. lemon oil polish   B. neatsfoot oil
    C. paste wax   D. water-emulsion wax

23. The use of concentrated acid to remove stains from ceramic tile bathroom floors USU-   23.____
ALLY results in making the surface

    A. pitted and porous   B. clean and shiny
    C. harder and glossier   D. waterproof

24. Asphalt tile floors should be protected by coating with   24.____

    A. hard-milled soap   B. water-emulsion wax
    C. sodium metaphosphate   D. varnish

25. Of the following, the BEST way to economize on cleaning tools and materials is to   25.____

    A. train the cleaners to use them properly
    B. order at least a three-year supply of every item in order to avoid annual price
       increase
    C. attach a price sticker to every item so that the people using them will realize their
       high cost
    D. delay ordering material for three months at the beginning of each year to be sure
       that the old material is used to the fullest extent

KEY (CORRECT ANSWERS)

1.	B	11.	D
2.	D	12.	C
3.	C	13.	A
4.	A	14.	A
5.	C	15.	D
6.	B	16.	B
7.	C	17.	C
8.	D	18.	A
9.	A	19.	C
10.	A	20.	A

21.	B
22.	C
23.	A
24.	B
25.	A

———

TEST 2

DIRECTIONS: Each question or incomplete statement is followed by several suggested answers or completions. Select the one that BEST answers the question or completes the statement. *PRINT THE LETTER OF THE CORRECT ANSWER IN THE SPACE AT THE RIGHT.*

1. Of the following office cleaning jobs performed during the year, the one which should be done MOST frequently is   1.____

    A. cleaning the fluorescent lights
    B. dusting the Venetian blinds
    C. cleaning the bookcase glass
    D. carpetsweeping the rug

2. The BEST polishing agent to use on wood furniture is   2.____

    A. pumice
    B. paste wax
    C. water emulsion wax
    D. neatsfoot oil

3. Lemon oil polish is used BEST to polish   3.____

    A. exterior bronze
    B. marble walls
    C. leather seats
    D. lacquered metal

4. Cleaning with trisodium phosphate is MOST likely to damage   4.____

    A. toilet bowls
    B. drain pipes
    C. polished marble floors
    D. rubber tile floors

5. Of the following cleaning agents, the one which should NOT be used to remove stains from urinals is   5.____

    A. caustic lye
    B. detergent
    C. oxalic acid
    D. muriatic acid

6. The one of the following cleaners which GENERALLY contains an abrasive is   6.____

    A. caustic lye
    B. trisodium phosphate
    C. scouring powder
    D. ammonia

7. The instructions on a box of cleaning powder say: *Mix one pound of cleaning powder in four gallons of water.* According to these instructions, how many ounces of cleaning powder should be mixed in one gallon of water?   7.____

    A. 4   B. 8   C. 12   D. 16

8. In accordance with recommended practice, a dust mop, when not being used, should be stored   8.____

    A. hanging, handle end down
    B. hanging, handle end up
    C. standing on the floor, handle end down
    D. standing on the floor, handle end up

9. The two types of floors found in public buildings are classified as hard floors and soft floors.
An example of a hard floor is one made of

    A. linoleum   B. cork
    C. ceramic tile   D. asphalt tile

9.____

10. A squeegee is a tool that is MAINLY used to clean

    A. painted walls   B. radiator covers
    C. window glass   D. ceramic tile floors

10.____

11. The BEST way to determine whether a cleaner is doing his work well is by

    A. observing the cleaner at work for several hours
    B. asking the cleaner questions about the work
    C. asking other cleaners to rate his work
    D. inspecting the cleanliness of the spaces assigned to the cleaner

11.____

12. The PRIMARY purpose of using a disinfectant material is to

    A. kill germs   B. destroy odors
    C. remove stains   D. kill insects

12.____

13. Windows should be washed by using a solution of warm water mixed with

    A. chlorine bleach   B. kerosene
    C. ammonia   D. soft soap

13.____

14. Of the following, the MOST effective way to reduce waste of cleaning tools is to

    A. keep careful records of how often tools are issued
    B. require that the old tool be returned before issuing a new one
    C. require that all tools be used for a fixed number of hours before replacing them
    D. train the cleaners to use the tools properly

14.____

15. The number of square feet of unobstructed corridor floor space that a cleaner should sweep in an hour is MOST NEARLY

    A. 1200   B. 2400   C. 4000   D. 6000

15.____

16. Sweeping compound is used on concrete floors MAINLY to

    A. polish the floor
    B. keep the dust down
    C. soften the encrusted dirt
    D. provide a non-slip surface

16.____

17. The BEST attachment to use on an electric scrubbing machine when stripping waxed resilient flooring is a

    A. nylon disk   B. soft brush
    C. steel wool pad   D. pumice wheel

17.____

18. A counter brush is BEST suited to cleaning

    A. water cooler drains   B. radiators
    C. light fixtures   D. lavatory fixtures

18.____

19. In high dusting of walls and ceilings, the CORRECT procedure is to　　　19._____

    A. begin with lower walls and process up to the ceiling
    B. remove pictures and window shades only if they are dusty
    C. clean the windows thoroughly before dusting any other part of the room
    D. begin with the ceiling, then dust the walls

20. When cleaning a room, the cleaner should　　　20._____

    A. dust desks before sweeping
    B. dust desks after sweeeping
    C. open windows wide during the desk dusting process
    D. begin dusting at rows most distant from entrance door

21. Too much water on asphalt tile is objectionable MAINLY because the tile　　　21._____

    A. will tend to become discolored or spotted
    B. may be loosened from the floor
    C. will be softened and made uneven
    D. colors will tend to run

22. To reduce the slip hazard resulting from waxing linoleum, the MOST practical of the fol-　　　22._____
lowing methods is

    A. apply the wax in one heavy coat
    B. apply the wax after varnishing the linoleum
    C. buff the wax surface thoroughly
    D. apply the wax in several thin coats

23. Assume that the water emulsion wax needed for routine waxing in your building is 15 gal-　　　23._____
lons per month. This wax is supplied in 55-gallon drums.
To cover your needs for a year, the MINIMUM number of drums you would have to
request is

    A. two   B. three   C. four   D. six

24. In washing down the walls, the correct procedure is to start at the bottom of the wall and　　　24._____
work to the top.
The MOST important reason for this is:

    A. Dirt streaking will tend to be avoided or easily removed
    B. Less cleansing agent will be required
    C. Rinse water will not be required
    D. The time for cleaning the wall is less than if washing started at the top of the wall

25. In mopping a wood floor, the cleaner should　　　25._____

    A. mop against the grain of the wood wherever possible
    B. mop as large an area as possible at one time
    C. wet the floor before mopping with a cleaning agent
    D. mop only aisles and clear areas and use a scrub brush under desks and chairs

KEY (CORRECT ANSWERS)

1.	D		11.	D
2.	B		12.	A
3.	A		13.	C
4.	C		14.	D
5.	D		15.	D
6.	C		16.	B
7.	A		17.	A
8.	B		18.	B
9.	C		19.	D
10.	C		20.	B

21.	B
22.	D
23.	C
24.	A
25.	C

———

TEST 3

DIRECTIONS: Each question or incomplete statement is followed by several suggested answers or completions. Select the one that BEST answers the question or completes the statement. *PRINT THE LETTER OF THE CORRECT ANSWER IN THE SPACE AT THE RIGHT.*

1. The MAIN reason for using a sweeping compound is to

    A. spot-finish waxed surfaces
    B. retard dust when sweeping floors
    C. loosen accumulations of grease
    D. remove paint spots from tile flooring

1.____

2. The one of the following cleaning agents which is recommended for use on marble floors is

    A. an acid cleaner
    B. a soft soap
    C. trisodium phosphate
    D. a neutral liquid detergent

2.____

3. A cleaning solution of one cup of soap chips dissolved in a pail of warm water can be used to wash

    A. painted walls   B. rubber tile
    C. marble walls   D. terrazzo floors

3.____

4. Sodium fluoride is a

    A. pesticide   B. disinfectant
    C. detergent   D. paint thinner

4.____

5. Scratches or burns in linoleum, rubber tile, or cork floors should be removed by rubbing with

    A. crocus cloth   B. fine steel wool
    C. sandpaper   D. emery cloth

5.____

6. A room 12 feet wide by 25 feet long has a floor area of _____ square feet.

    A. 37   B. 200   C. 300   D. 400

6.____

7. A cleaning solution should be applied to a painted wall using a

    A. wool rag   B. brush   C. sponge   D. squeegee

7.____

8. When scrubbing a wooden floor, it is ADVISABLE to

    A. flood the surface with the cleaning solution in order to float the dirt out of all cracks and crevices
    B. hose off the loosened dirt before starting the scrubbing operation
    C. pick up the cleaning solution as soon as possible
    D. mix a mild acid with the cleaning solution in order to clean the surface quickly

8.____

9. How many hours will it take a worker to sweep a floor space of 2800 square feet if he sweeps at the of 800 square feet per hour?   9.____

    A. 8   B. $6\frac{1}{2}$ C. $3\frac{1}{2}$ D. $2\frac{1}{2}$

10. One gallon of water contains   10.____

    A. 2 quarts   B. 4 quarts   C. 2 pints   D. 4 pints

11. A standard cleaning solution is prepared by mixing 4 ounces of detergent powder in 2 gallons of water. The number of ounces of detergent powder needed for the same strength solution in 5 gallons of water is   11.____

    A. 4   B. 6   C. 8   D. 10

12. The principal reason why soap should NOT be used in cleaning windows is   12.____

    A. it causes loosening of the putty
    B. it may cause rotting of the wood frames
    C. a film is left on the window, requiring additional rinsing
    D. frequent use of soap will cause the glass to become permanently clouded

13. When a window pane is broken, the FIRST step the custodian takes is to   13.____

    A. remove broken glass from floors and the window sill
    B. determine the cause
    C. remove the putty with a putty knife
    D. prepare a piece of glass to replace the broken pane

14. Your instructions to a cleaner about the proper sweeping of offices should include the following Instruction: 14.____

    A. Do not move chairs and wastebaskets from their places when sweeping
    B. Place chairs and baskets on the desks to get them out of the way
    C. Set aside the loose small furniture and chairs in an orderly manner when sweeping office floors
    D. Move the desks and chairs to the side of the room close to the wall in order to sweep properly

15. To remove dirt accumulations after the completion of the sweeping task, brushes should be   15.____

    A. tapped on the floor in the normal sweeping position
    B. struck on the floor against the side of the block
    C. struck on the floor against the end of the block
    D. turned upside down and the handle tapped on the floor

16. To sweep rough cement floors in a basement, the BEST tool to use is a   16.____

    A. deck brush   B. new 30" floor brush
    C. corn broom   D. treated mop

17. When a floor is scrubbed, it is NOT correct to   17.____

    A. use a steady, even rotary motion
    B. rinse the floor with clean hot water
    C. have the mop strokes follow the boards when drying the floor
    D. wet the floor first by pouring several bucketsful of water on it

18. Flushing with a hose is MOST appropriate as a method of cleaning   18.____

    A. terrazzo floors of corridors
    B. untreated wood floors
    C. linoleum floors where not in frequent use
    D. cement floors

19. Improper use of a carbon dioxide type portable fire extinguisher may cause injury to the   19.____
    operator because

    A. handling the nozzle during discharge can cause frostbite to the skin
    B. carbon dioxide is highly poisonous if breathed into the lungs
    C. use of carbon dioxide on an oil fire can cause a chemical explosion
    D. the powdery residue left by the discharge is highly caustic to the skin

20. When using a portable single ladder with ten rungs, the GREATEST number of rungs   20.____
    that a cleaner should climb up is

    A. 7   B. 8   C. 9   D. 10

21. Of the following types of portable fire extinguishers, the one which should be used to   21.____
    control a fire in or around live electrical equipment is the _____ type.

    A. foam   B. soda acid
    C. carbon dioxide   D. gas cartridge water

22. The MOST frequent cause of accidental injuries to workers on the job is   22.____

    A. unsafe working practices of employees
    B. poor design of buildings and working areas
    C. lack of warning signs in hazardous work areas
    D. lack of adequate safety guards on equipment and machinery

23. Of the following, the MOST important purpose of preparing an accident report on an   23.____
    injury to a cleaner is to help

    A. collect statistics on different types of accidents
    B. calm the feelings of the injured cleaner
    C. prevent similar accidents in the future
    D. prove that the cleaner was at fault

24. The one of the following types of locks that is used on emergency exit doors is the   24.____
    _____ bolt.

    A. panic   B. dead   C. cinch   D. toggle

25. The one of the following types of locks that USUALLY contains both a live bolt and a dead bolt is a _____ lock.

   25._____

   A. mortise
   C. loose pin butt
                           B. double-hung window
                           D. window frame

KEY (CORRECT ANSWERS)

1.	B		11.	D	
2.	D		12.	C	
3.	A		13.	A	
4.	A		14.	C	
5.	B		15.	A	
6.	C		16.	C	
7.	C		17.	D	
8.	C		18.	D	
9.	C		19.	A	
10.	B		20.	B	

21. C
22. A
23. C
24. A
25. A

EXAMINATION SECTION
TEST 1

DIRECTIONS: Each question or incomplete statement is followed by several suggested answers or completions. Select the one that BEST answers the question or completes the statement. *PRINT THE LETTER OF THE CORRECT ANSWER IN THE SPACE AT THE RIGHT.*

1. The BEST technique to use when washing the outside surface of the upper sash of double-hung windows that are not equipped with safety belt anchors is to work from a   1.____

    A. standing position on the outside of the sill
    B. sitting position on the sill with the feet inside the room
    C. standing position on the inside of the sill
    D. standing position on the top of a stepladder

2. The use of trisodium phosphate in cleaning marble should be avoided because   2.____

    A. it discolors the surface of the marble
    B. the salt crystals get in the pores, expand and crack the marble
    C. it pits the glazed surface and bleaches the marble
    D. it builds up a slick surface on the marble

3. The use of a concentrated cleaning solution on painted or varnished woodwork   3.____

    A. results in burning the pigments of paint or varnish, causing dull, streaky surfaces
    B. cuts down on time and energy in maintaining clean, unblemished surfaces
    C. insures spotless, clean, bright surfaces
    D. is detrimental to the health of the cleaners

4. Employees engaged in cleaning operations who are issued rubber gloves to protect their hands against caustic solutions should be warned that   4.____

    A. such solution allowed to spill over the glove top into the space between the glove and the hand may damage the skin of the hand
    B. rubber gloves have a very short life in contact with caustic solutions
    C. harmful gases can penetrate the rubber and harm even dry hands
    D. contact of the hands with glove-type rubber for over an hour is harmful

5. Pyrethrins are used as   5.____

    A. insecticides   B. germicides
    C. waxes   D. detergents

6. A cleaning solution is made up of 4 gallons of water, 1 pint of liquid soap, and 1 pint of ammonia.   6.____
   How many gallons of water is needed to use up a gallon of ammonia?

    A. 8   B. 16   C. 24   D. 32

7. Suppose a cleaner has 50 stair halls to clean.   7.____
   If he cleans 74% of them, the number of stair halls still UNCLEANED is

    A. 38   B. 26   C. 24   D. 13

8. The prevention and control of vermin and rodents in a school building is PRIMARILY a matter of

    8.___

    A. maintaining good housekeeping on a continuous basis
    B. periodic use of an exterminator's service
    C. calling in the exterminator when necessary
    D. cleaning the building thoroughly during school vacation

9. Of the following, the LEAST desirable agent for cleaning blackboards is

    9.___

    A. damp cloth
    B. clear warm water applied with a sponge
    C. warm water with a little kerosene
    D. warm water containing a mild soap solution

10. Chalk trays of blackboards should be washed and cleaned

    10.___

    A. once a week
    B. daily
    C. only when the teacher reports cleaning needed
    D. once a month

11. In cleaning rooms by means of a central vacuum cleaning system,

    11.___

    A. sweeping compound is used merely to prevent dust from rising
    B. rooms need cleaning only twice a week because the machine takes up the oil
    C. wood floors must be oiled more frequently as the machine takes up the oil
    D. the cleaner should not press down upon the tool but should guide it across the floor

Questions 12-14.

DIRECTIONS: Questions 12 through 14 are to be answered on the basis of the followimng passage.

Terrazzo flooring will last a very long time if it is cared for properly. Lacquers, shellac or varnish preparations should never be used on terrazzo. Soap cleaners are not recommended since they dull the appearance of the floor. Alkaline solutions are harmful, so a neutral cleaner or non-alkaline synthetic detergents will give best results. If the floor is very dirty, it may be necessary to scrub it. Them same neutral cleaning solution should be used for scrubbing as for mopping. Scouring powder may be sprinkled at particularly dirty spots. Do not use steel wool for scrubbing. Small pieces of steel filings left on the floor will rust and discolor the terrazzo. Non-woven or open-mesh fabric abrasive pads are suitable for scrubbing terrazzo floors.

12. According to the above passage, the BEST cleaning agent for terrazzo flooring is a(n)

    12.___

    A. soap cleaner
    B. varnish preparations
    C. neutral cleaner
    D. alkaline solution

13. According to the above passage, terrazzo floors should NOT be scrubbed with

    13.___

    A. non-woven nylon abrasive pads
    B. steel wool
    C. open-mesh febric abrasive pads
    D. scouring powder

14. As used in the above passage, the word *discolor* means MOST NEARLY

    A. crack   B. scratch
    C. dissolve   D. stain

14.____

15. New installations of vinyl tile floors should

    A. never be machine scrubbed
    B. be dry buffed weekly
    C. be swept daily, using an oily compound
    D. never be swept with treated dust mops

15.____

16. Scalers for open-grained wood floors should NOT contain linseed oil because

    A. the linseed oil would damage the wood fibers
    B. the linseed oil would deteriorate mop strands
    C. water wax would penetrate the linseed oil sealer and rot the wood
    D. linseed oil on wood takes too long to dry satisfactorily before a floor finish could be applied

16.____

17. When washing painted wall areas by hand, a man should be expected to wash each hour an area, in square feet, equal to

    A. 75-125   B. 150-300
    C. 400-600   D. 750-1000

17.____

18. Of the following, the one that is MOST desirable to use in dusting furniture is a

    A. feather duster   B. paper towel
    C. counter brush   D. soft cotton cloth

18.____

19. The one of the following floor types on which oily sweeping compound may be used is

    A. vinyl tile   B. concrete
    C. linoleum   D. terrazzo

19.____

20. Which of the following is the PROPER method of cleaning a room?

    A. Dust, empty wastebasket, sweep
    B. Empty wastebasket, dust, sweep
    C. Empty wastebasket, sweep, dust
    D. Sweep, dust, empty wastebasket

20.____

21. How would you determine when a waxed floor should be stripped?
When

    A. someone slipped on the floor
    B. wax builds up
    C. scuffs are not removed by buffing
    D. someone complains

21.____

22. To remove modelling plaster from the floor, you should use

    A. a sharp chisel
    B. a putty knife
    C. a floor scrubbing machine
    D. sulphuric acid

22.____

23. Which of the following floors would you NOT seal?

    A. Terrazzo   B. Cork   C. Asphalt   D. Tile

23.____

24. When vacuum cleaning rugs, the suction tool should be pushed _____ the lay of the nap.

    A. diagonally across   B. with
    C. across   D. against

24.____

25. Of the following, the use for which central vacuum cleaning is considered LEAST effective is for

    A. cleaning walls and ceilings
    B. dusting classroom furniture
    C. cleaning boiler rooms
    D. cleaning erasers

25.____

KEY(CORRECT ANSWERS)

1.	B		11.	D
2.	B		12.	C
3.	A		13.	B
4.	A		14.	D
5.	A		15.	B
6.	D		16.	D
7.	D		17.	B
8.	A		18.	D
9.	C		19.	B
10.	A		20.	C

21.	B
22.	B
23.	C
24.	B
25.	B

TEST 2

DIRECTIONS: Each question or incomplete statement is followed by several suggested answers or completions. Select the one that BEST answers the question or completes the statement. *PRINT THE LETTER OF THE CORRECT ANSWER IN THE SPACE AT THE RIGHT.*

1. A garage broom is USUALLY used to sweep
   - A. small asphalt walks
   - C. small cement walks
   - B. playgrounds
   - D. incinerator rooms

1.____

2. Listed below are the first four steps to follow when you are dusting furniture:
   - I. Move objects on furniture and dust under them
   - II. Refold cloth
   - III. Dust furniture itself
   - IV. Fold the dusting cloth

   The CORRECT order of these steps should be:
   - A. I, IV, III, II
   - C. IV, II, I, III
   - B. III, IV, II, I
   - D. IV, III, II, I

2.____

3. Snow removal should begin
   - A. after the snow has been packed solid
   - B. as soon as possible
   - C. when the depth is more than 2 inches
   - D. when the weather bureau says it is a *heavy snowfall*

3.____

4. On which of the following should you advise a cleaner to use a corn broom?
   - A. Basement areas
   - C. Rubber tile floors
   - B. Stair halls
   - D. Window sills

4.____

5. Of the following, the BEST material to use to clean exterior bronze is
   - A. pumice
   - B. paste wax
   - C. wire wheel on portable buffer
   - D. lemon oil polish

5.____

6. The floor area, in square feet, on which a properly treated dustless sweeping cloth can be used before the cloth must be washed is
   - A. 500-1000
   - B. 2000-300
   - C. 4000-6000
   - D. 8000-10000

6.____

7. A cleaning woman working a six-hour shift should be able to cover (clean) _____ Gilbert work units.
   - A. 100-200
   - B. 400-500
   - C. 1100-1200
   - D. 6000-7000

7.____

8. The following tasks are frequently done when an office is cleaned:
   - I. The floor is vacuumed
   - II. The ashtrays and wastebaskets are emptied
   - III. The desks and furniture are dusted

   The order in which these tasks should GENERALLY be done is:
   - A. I, II, III
   - C. III, II, I
   - B. II, III, I
   - D. I, III, II

8.____

9. When wax is applied to a floor by the use of a twine mop with handle, the wax should be _____ with the mop.   9.___

   A. applied in thin coats
   B. applied in heavy coats
   C. poured on the floor, then spread
   D. dropped on the floor, then spread

10. The BEST way to clean dust from an acoustical-type ceiling is with a   10.___

   A. strong soap solution   B. wet sponge
   C. vacuum cleaner   D. stream of water

11. The fan motor in a central vacuum cleaner system is found to be operating at 110% of its rated capacity.   11.___
The one of the following actions which is MOST likely to decrease the load on the motor is

   A. tying-back several outlets in the open position on each floor
   B. moving the butterfly damper slightly toward the closed position
   C. removing ten percent of the filter bags
   D. operating the bag shaker continuously

12. A groundskeeper asks how to remove an accumulation of grease from the concrete near the loading dock.   12.___
Of the following, the cleaning agent that a custodian should tell him to use to degrease the area is a(n)

   A. acid cleaner   B. alkaline cleaner
   C. liquid soap   D. solvent cleaner

13. The instructions for mixing a powdered cleaner in water state: *Mix three ounces of powder in a 14-quart pail three-quarters full of water.* A cleaner asks you how much powdered cleaner he should use in a mop truck containing 28 gallons of water to obtain the same strength solution.   13.___
Your answer should be _____ ounces of powder.

   A. 6   B. 8   C. 24   D. 32

14. The type of soft floor that is basically a mixture of oxidized linseed oil, resin, and ground cork pressed upon a burlap backing is known as   14.___

   A. asphalt tile   B. cork tile
   C. linoleum   D. vinyl tile

15. The difficulty of cleaning soil from surfaces is LEAST affected by the   15.___

   A. length of time between cleanings
   B. chemical nature of the soil
   C. smoothness of the surface being cleaned
   D. standard time allotted to the job

16. The one of the following cleaning agents that is GENERALLY classified as an alkaline cleaner is   16.____

    A. sodium carbonate   B. ground silica
    C. kerosene   D. lemon oil

17. The one of the following cleaning agents that should be used ONLY when adequate ventilation and protective measures have been taken is   17.____

    A. methylene chloride   B. sodium chloride
    C. sodium carbonate   D. calcium carbonate

18. Of the following, the MOST important consideration in the selection of a cleaning agent is the   18.____

    A. cost per pound or gallon
    B. amount of labor involved in its use
    C. wording of the manufacturer's warranty
    D. length of time the manufacturer has been producing cleaning agents

19. Which of the following statements about sweeping is NOT correct?   19.____

    A. Corridors and stairs should not be swept during school hours.
    B. Classrooms should usually be swept daily after the close of the afternoon session.
    C. Dry sweeping is not to be used in classrooms or corridors.
    D. Special rooms, as sewing rooms, may be swept during school hours, if unoccupied.

20. The PROPER size of floor brush to be used in classrooms with fixed seats is _____ inches.   20.____

    A. 36   B. 24   C. 16   D. 6

21. Sweeping compound made of oiled sawdust should NOT be used on _____ floors.   21.____

    A. cement   B. rubber tile
    C. oiled wood   D. composition

22. In oiling a wood floor, it is good practice to   22.____

    A. apply the oil with a dipped mop up to the baseboards of the walls
    B. avoid application of oil closer then 6 inches of the baseboards
    C. keep the oil about one inch from the baseboard
    D. make sure that oil is applied to the floors under radiators

23. The BEST reason why water should not be used to clean kalsomined walls of a boiler room is that the   23.____

    A. walls are usually not smooth and will hold too much water
    B. kalsomine coating does not hold dust
    C. kalsomine coating will dissolve in water and leave streaks
    D. wall brick and kalsomine coating will not dissolve in water and so cannot be cleaned

24. In mopping a floor, it is BEST practice to

    24._____

   A. swing the mop from side to side, using the widest possible stroke across the floor up to the baseboard
   B. swing the mop from side to side, using the widest possible stroke across the floor surface, stopping the stroke from 3 to 5 inches from baseboards
   C. use short, straight strokes, up and back, stopping the strokes about 5 inches from the baseboards
   D. use short, straight strokes, up and back, stopping the strokes at the baseboard

25. A teacher tells you that waxing a rubber tile floor is dangerous because the floor becomes too slippery. Your response should be

    25._____

   A. that the children should be careful in walking on these floors and should wear rubber heels to avoid slipping
   B. an explanation of the non-slipping properties of a water emulsion wax properly applied
   C. tell her to mind her own business
   D. that It is not dangerous because no children have fallen and injured themselves

---

KEY(CORRECT ANSWERS)

1.	B		11.	B
2.	D		12.	D
3.	B		13.	D
4.	A		14.	C
5.	D		15.	D
6.	C		16.	A
7.	C		17.	A
8.	B		18.	B
9.	A		19.	A
10.	C		20.	C

21.	B
22.	D
23.	C
24.	B
25.	B

TEST 3

DIRECTIONS: Each question or Incomplete statement is followed by several suggested answers or completions. Select the one that BEST answers the question or completes the statement. *PRINT THE LETTER OF THE CORRECT ANSWER IN THE SPACE AT THE RIGHT.*

1. The KEY figure in any custodial safety program is the   1._____

   A. custodian   B. cleaner
   C. security officer   D. building manager

2. A custodian must inspect or have a maintenance man inspect every window cleaner's   2._____
   safety belt AT LEAST

   A. each time the windows are washed
   B. once a month
   C. once a year
   D. once every second year

3. A custodian's written instruction to his staff on the subject of security in public buildings   3._____
   should include instructions to

   A. exclude the public at all times
   B. admit the public at all times
   C. admit the public only if they are neat and well-dressed
   D. admit the public during specified hours

4. A custodian in charge of a building who is normally on duty during the daytime hours in a   4._____
   building which is cleaned at night should

   A. never make night inspections since he is not responsible for the cleanliness of the building
   B. make night inspections at least once a year
   C. never make night inspections because the cleaners will think he is spying on them
   D. make night inspections at least twice a month

5. The employee MOST likely to find the nests and runways of roaches and vermin in a   5._____
   building is a

   A. maintenance man   B. night cleaner
   C. building custodian   D. stationary fireman

6. When mopping, the pails containing the cleaning solutions should be   6._____

   A. slid along the floor to avoid injury due to lifting
   B. kept off the floor preferably on a rolling platform
   C. shifted from place to place using the mop
   D. equipped with a spigot for applying the mopping solution

7. Of the following, the item that is considered a concrete floor sealer is   7._____

   A. water wax   B. sodium hypochlorite
   C. sodium silicate   D. linseed oil

8. To order wet mop filler replacements, a custodian should specify the   8.____

    A. number of strands   B. girth
    C. weight   D. wet test strength

9. One day a cleaner said to his foreman, *I can get a tile cleaner that is as good as the stuff*   9.____
we use and for less money because my brother is a building contractor. How about it?
The CORRECT way for the foreman to handle this situation is for him to

    A. thank the cleaner but tell him that individual cleaners cannot buy their own cleaning material for project use
    B. tell the cleaner that no one has any right to start interfering in the buying procedures of the housing authority
    C. go along with the cleaner and buy the cleaner from his brother because it might save money for the authority
    D. tell the cleaner to have his brother contact the project manager

10. A new cleaner under your supervision is waxing a floor for the first time. While the job   10.____
seems to be going along well, he is not doing it quite the way you asked him to do it and
so is taking longer than he should.
Which of the following is the BEST action for you to take under these conditions?

    A. Leave him to finish the Job and go on to the next one.
    B. Interrupt him and tell him to do the job the way he was taught.
    C. Tell him he is doing well but that he should do better.
    D. Explain to him why your way is faster and tell him to try it.

11. The EASIEST way to find out how many supplies you have available is for you to   11.____

    A. look at last year's figures
    B. keep an up-to-date inventory
    C. ask one of your men to let you know
    D. check the availability when you use a special item

12. The BEST way to remove chewing gum from the floor is with a   12.____

    A. cloth wet with acid   B. bristle brush
    C. putty knife   D. rubber sponge

13. The 16-inch hair broom is BEST on   13.____

    A. basement areas   B. cement walks
    C. stair risers   D. stair halls

14. It is MOST important that the slot in the floor saddle of the elevator be kept free of dirt   14.____
since, otherwise,

    A. a fire may start
    B. it will be unsightly
    C. someone may slip
    D. the door will not close

15. Wall panels in elevators should be cleaned with a cloth dipped in   15.____

    A. ammonia in water   B. gasoline
    C. hot water   D. neutral soap solution

16. The legal minimum age of employees engaged for cleaning windows in the state is _____ years.

    A. 16   B. 17   C. 18   D. 21

16._____

17. Wood and cork floors should be sealed because

    A. these surfaces have tiny natural openings that can trap dirt and grease
    B. it keeps these kinds of floors from warping and buckling
    C. it makes the surface stronger
    D. the sealing process makes the surface easier to walk on

17._____

18. A single 8-foot ladder is to be used for a certain window washing job. Of the distances from the wall which are given below, which one is BEST to place the ladder from the wall?
_____ feet.

    A. 2   B. 4   C. 6   D. 8

18._____

19. To lift something without injury to yourself, you should obey all of the following rules EXCEPT:

    A. Keep your back straight
    B. Get help with heavy loads
    C. Lift quickly with your arms
    D. Stand close to what you are lifting

19._____

20. The type of product to use when cleaning asphalt tile is

    A. sandpaper pad   B. plain ammonia
    C. water base wax   D. oil base polish

20._____

21. When you are taking a mop outfit with wringer through a corridor, it is very important to proceed slowly past

    A. you might slip and hurt yourself
    B. you should look for any cracks in the floor
    C. you must watch out for people who might come through the doorway
    D. the doorway area is more slippery than the rest of the corridor

21._____

22. Which one of the following is the MOST important piece of clothing to wear while cleaning an incinerator?

    A. Leather boots   B. Fireman's helmet
    C. Heavy coat   D. Work gloves

22._____

23. Of the following, who should hang the elevator pads to be used when tenants move in or out?
The

    A. foreman
    B. tenant himself
    C. cleaner assigned to the building
    D. elevator mechanic

23._____

24. The floor that should NOT be machined scrubbed is a(n)   24.____

    A. lobby   B. lunchroom
    C. gymnasium   D. auditorium aisle

25. Pick-up sweeping in a busy building is the occasional removal of the more conspicuous   25.____
loose dirt from corridors and lobbies.
This type of sweeping should be done

    A. after scrubbing or waxing of floors
    B. with the aid of a sweeping compound
    C. at night after hours
    D. during regular hours

KEY (CORRECT ANSWERS)

1.	A		11.	B
2.	C		12.	C
3.	D		13.	D
4.	D		14.	D
5.	B		15.	A
6.	B		16.	C
7.	C		17.	A
8.	C		18.	A
9.	A		19.	C
10.	D		20.	C

21.	C
22.	D
23.	C
24.	C
25.	D

EXAMINATION SECTION
TEST 1

DIRECTIONS: Each question or incomplete statement is followed by several suggested answers or completions. Select the one that BEST answers the question or completes the statement. *PRINT THE LETTER OF THE CORRECT ANSWER IN THE SPACE AT THE RIGHT.*

1. Washing soda is used to   1._____

    A.   eliminate the need for rinse mopping or wiping
    B.   make the cleaning compound abrasive
    C.   decrease the wetting power of water
    D.   increase the wetting power of water

2. Varnish or lacquer may be used as a sealer on floors finished with   2._____

    A.   asphalt tiles   B.   linoleum
    C.   rubber tiles   D.   cork tiles

3. A long-handled deck scrub brush is MOST effective when scrubbing   3._____

    A.   large open areas   B.   stair treads
    C.   small flat areas   D.   long corridors

4. The BEST method for preventing the infestation of a building by rats is to   4._____

    A.   use cats
    B.   use rat traps
    C.   eliminate rat harborages in the building
    D.   use poisoned bait

5. The one of the following which is NOT recommended for prolonging the useful life of a   5._____
hair broom is to

    A.   rotate the brush to avoid wear on one side only
    B.   wash the brush by using It as a mop once a week
    C.   comb the brush weekly
    D.   hang the brush In storage to avoid resting on bristles

6. A good indication of the quality of the cleaning operation in a building is the   6._____

    A.   amount of cleaning material used each month
    B.   number of cleaners employed
    C.   number of complaints of unsanitary conditions received
    D.   number of square feet of hall space cleaned daily

7. Spontaneous ignition is MOST likely to occur in a   7._____

    A.   pile of oily rags
    B.   vented fuel oil tank
    C.   metal file cabinet filled with papers in file folders
    D.   covered metal container containing clean rags

8. The MOST important reason for oiling wood floors is that 8.____

    A. it keeps the dust from rising during the sweeping process
    B. the need for daily sweeping of classroom floors is eliminated
    C. oiled floors present a better appearance than waxed floors
    D. the wood surface will become waterproof and stain-proof

9. After oil has been sprayed on a wood floor, the sprayed should be cleaned before storing it. 9.____
    The USUAL cleaning material for this purpose is

    A. ammonia water   B. salt
    C. kerosene   D. alcohol

10. It is usually desirable to assign the cleaning of an office to one employee only because 10.____

    A. the amount of time wasted through talking is decreased
    B. an employee working alone, by himself, is more efficient
    C. there is no question who is responsible for the work done
    D. working alone reduces the rate and severity of accidents

11. Of each dollar spent on the cleaning of public buildings, the amount spent on cleaning supplies is USUALLY not more than _____ cents. 11.____

    A. 5   B. 35   C. 55   D. 75

12. Cleansing powders such as Ajax should NOT be used to clean and polish brass MAINLY because 12.____

    A. the brass turns a much darker color
    B. such cleaners have no effect on tarnish
    C. the surface of the brass may become scratched
    D. too much fine dust is raised in the polishing process

13. To remove chalk marks on sidewalks and cemented playground areas, the MOST acceptable cleaning method is 13.____

    A. using a brush with warm water
    B. using a brush with warm water containing some kerosene
    C. hosing down such areas with water
    D. using a brush with a solution of muriatic acid in water

14. Of the following solutions, the one MOST often used in washing exterior glass is _____ water and a small quantity of _____. 14.____

    A. hot; turpentine   B. cold; ammonia
    C. cold; glass wax   D. warm; soft soap

15. Rust stains in wash basins can BEST be prevented by 15.____

    A. applying wax film to the rusty surface
    B. replacing leaking faucet washers
    C. adding rust inhibitor to the domestic cold water storage tank
    D. sandpapering the rusty surfaces

16. Of the following, the one which is likely to be MOST harmful to asphalt tile is   16.____

    A. coffee   B. ketchup   C. salad oil   D. vinegar

17. Of the following, when sweeping a corridor with a floor brush, the cleaner should   17.____

    A. lean on the brush and walk the length of the corridor
    B. give the brush a slight jerk after each stroke to free it of loose dirt
    C. make certain there is no overlap on sweeping strokes
    D. use moderately long pull strokes

18. Time standards for cleaning are of value ONLY if   18.____

    A. a bonus is promised if the time standards are beaten
    B. the cleaners determine the methods and procedures to be used
    C. accompanied by a completely detailed description of the methods to be used
    D. a schematic diagram of the area is made available to the cleaners

19. In using a floor brush in a corridor, a cleaner should be instructed to   19.____

    A. use moderately long pull strokes whenever possible
    B. make certain that there is no overlap on sweeping strokes
    C. give the brush a slight jerk alter each stroke to free it of loose dirt
    D. keep the sweeping surface of the brush firmly flat on the floor to obtain maximum coverage

20. Of the following, the BEST procedure in sweeping classroom floors is: 20.____

    A. Open all windows before beginning the sweeping operation
    B. The cleaner should move forward while sweeping
    C. Alternate pull and push strokes should be used
    D. sweep under desks on both sides of an aisle while moving down the aisle

21. PROPER care of floor brushes includes   21.____

    A. washing brushes daily after each use with warm soap solution
    B. dipping brushes in kerosene periodically to remove dirt
    C. washing with warm soap solution at least once a month
    D. avoiding contact with soap or soda solutions to prevent drying of bristles

22. An ADVANTAGE of vacuum cleaning rather than sweeping a floor with a floor brush is: 22.____

    A. Stationary furniture will not be touched by the cleaning tool
    B. The problem of dust on furniture is reduced
    C. The initial cost of the apparatus is less than the cost of an equivalent number of floor brushes
    D. Daily sweeping of rooms and corridors can be eliminated

23. Sweeping compound for use on rubber tiles, asphalt tile, or sealed wood floors must NOT contain   23.____

    A. sawdust   B. water   C. oil soap   D. floor oil

24. The one of the following cleaning operations for which a custodian is LEAST likely to use vacuum cleaning equipment is   24.____

    A. cleaning blackboard erasers
    B. removing dust from blinds or draperies
    C. cleaning toilet room floors
    D. high dusting of classroom walls

25. In mopping the wood floor of a classroom, it is considered BEST practice to   25.____

    A. mop as large an area as possible before rinsing
    B. mop across the grain wherever possible
    C. sweep the floor thoroughly before mopping
    D. start mopping in the front of the room nearest the door entrance

---

KEY (CORRECT ANSWERS)

1.	D		11.	A
2.	D		12.	C
3.	C		13.	A
4.	C		14.	B
5.	B		15.	B
6.	C		16.	C
7.	A		17.	B
8.	A		18.	C
9.	C		19.	C
10.	C		20.	A

21.	C
22.	B
23.	D
24.	C
25.	C

40

TEST 2

DIRECTIONS: Each question or incomplete statement is followed by several suggested answers or completions. Select the one that BEST answers the question or completes the statement. *PRINT THE LETTER OF THE CORRECT ANSWER IN THE SPACE AT THE RIGHT.*

1. Of the following cleaning jobs to be done by hand, one cleaner should normally take the LONGEST time to finish a 1,000 square foot area when he is   1.____

   A. wet mopping a soft floor
   B. wasing a marble floor
   C. wet mopping a hard floor
   D. washing restroom tile

2. A cleaner takes an average of forty minutes to mop 1,000 square feet of floor. The amount of time this cleaner should take to mop the floor of a rectangular corridor eight feet wide by sixty feet long is, on the average, MOST NEARLY _____ minutes.   2.____

   A. 10   B. 20   C. 30   D. 40

3. By normal work standards, the time it should take a cleaner to clean ten toilet bowls is MOST NEARLY _____ minutes.   3.____

   A. 5   B. 10   C. 25   D. 50

4. An auditorium eighty feet by 100 feet must be swept in one hour. If each cleaner takes fifteen minutes to sweep 1,000 square feet of auditorium area, the number of cleaners that must be assigned to complete the sweeping in one hour is   4.____

   A. 1   B. 2   C. 3   D. 4

5. Under normal circumstances, the one of the following daily cleaning jobs which it is LEAST important to complete on a day when only half of your cleaners report for work is the   5.____

   A. cleaning of toilets   B. sweeping of corridors
   C. collecting of trash   D. sweeping of stairs

6. A material COMMONLY used in detergents is   6.____

   A. rock salt   B. Glauber's salt
   C. trisodium phosphats   D. monosodium glutamate

7. A disinfectant material is one that will   7.____

   A. kill germs
   B. dissolve soil and stop odors
   C. give a clean odor and cover a disagreeable odor
   D. prevent soil buildup

8. When scrubbing a wooden floor, it is ADVISABLE to   8.____

   A. flood the surface with the cleaning solution in order to float the soil out of all crevices
   B. hose off the loosened soil before starting the scrubbing operation

C. pick up the used solution as soon as possible
D. mix a mild acid with the cleaning solution in order to clean the surface quickly

9. Before starting a wall washing operation, it is BEST to 9.____

    A. check the temperature of the water
    B. soak the sponge to be used
    C. check the pH of the mixed cleaning solution
    D. dust the wall to be washed

10. The device which Is LEAST likely to be used by the custodian in cleaning minor stop-pages in the plumbing system is a 10.____

    A. snake   B. auger   C. plunger   D. trowel

11. The first aid treatment for chemical burns on the skin is 11.____

    A. treatment with ointment and then bandaging
    B. washing with large quantities of water and then treating as heat burns
    C. treatment with a neutralizing agent and no bandaging
    D. application of sodium bicarbonate and then bandaging

12. The chemical MOST frequently used to clean drains clogged with grease is 12.____

    A. muriatic acid   B. soda ash
    C. ammonia   D. caustic soda

13. The one of the following terms which BEST describes the size of a water pail is 13.____

    A. 10 quart   B. 32 ounce
    C. 24 inch O.D.   D. 10 square feet

14. The one of the following terms which BEST describes the size of a floor scrubber brush is 14.____

    A. 10 quart   B. 32 ounce
    C. 24 inch O.D.   D. 10 square foot

15. Of the following items, the one which is BEST to use when dusting a mahogany table is a 15.____

    A. feather duster   B. treated cotton cloth
    C. crocus cloth   D. wet sponge

16. The one of the following tasks which should be a two-man assignment is 16.____

    A. vacuum cleaning a rug
    B. sweeping a classroom
    C. washing blackboards in a classroom
    D. washing fluorescent light fixtures

17. The BEST way to remove some small pieces of broken glass from a floor is to 17.____

    A. use a brush and dustpan
    B. pick up the pieces carefully with your hands
    C. use a wet mop and a wringer
    D. sweep the pieces into the corner of the room

18. There is a two-light fixture in the room where you are working. One of the lightbulbs goes   18.____
    out, and you need more light to work by.
    You should

    A. change the fuse in the fuse box
    B. have a new bulb put in
    C. call for an electrician and stop work until he comes
    D. find out what is causing the short circuit

19. While working on the job, you accidentally break a window pane. No one is around, and   19.____
    you are able to clean up the broken pieces of glass.
    It would then be BEST for you to

    A. leave a note near the window that a new glass has to be put in because it was acci-
       dentally broken
    B. forget about the whole thing because the window was not broken on purpose
    C. write a report to your supervisor telling him that you saw a broken window pane
       that has to be fixed
    D. tell your supervisor that you accidentally broke the window pane while working

Questions 20-23.

DIRECTIONS: Questions 20 through 23 are to be answered on the basis of the information
              given in the following passage.

MOPPING FLOORS

When mopping hardened cement floors, either painted or unpainted, a soap and water
mixture should be used. This should be made by dissolving half a cup of soft soap in a pail of
hot water. It is not desirable, however, under any circumstances, to use a soap and water mixture on cement floors that are not hardened. For mopping this type of floor. It is recommended that the cleaning agent be made up of 2 ounces of laundry soda mixed in a pail of
water.

Soaps are not generally used on hard tile floors because slippery films may build up on
the floor. It Is generally recommended that these floors be mopped using a pall of hot water in
which has been mixed 2 ounces of washing powder for each gallon of water. The floors
should then be rinsed thoroughly.

After the mopping is finished, proper care should be taken of the mop. This is done by
first cleaning the mop in clear warm water. Then it should be wrung out, after which the
strands of the mop should be untangled. Finally, the mop should be hung up by its handle to
dry.

20. According to the above passage, you should NEVER use a soap and water mixture when   20.____
    mopping _____ floors.

    A. hardened cement   B. painted
    C. unhardened cement   D. unpalnted

21. According to the above passage, using laundry soda mixed in a pail of water as a cleaning agent is recommended for   21.____

    A. all floors
    B. all floors except hard tile floors
    C. some cement floors
    D. linoleum floor coverings only

22. According to the above passage, the GENERALLY recommended mixture for mopping hard tile floors is _____ of hot water.   22.____

    A. 1/2 cup of soft soap for each gallon
    B. 1/2 cup of soft soap in a pail
    C. 2 ounces of washing powder in a pail
    D. 2 ounces of washing powder for each gallon

23. According to the above passage, the PROPER care of a mop after it is used includes   23.____

    A. cleaning it in clear cold water and hanging it by its handle to dry
    B. wringing it out, untangling, and drying it
    C. untangling its strands before wringing it out
    D. untangling its strands while cleaning it In clear water

24. The FIRST operation in routine cleaning of toilets and washrooms is to   24.____

    A. wash floors   B. clean walls
    C. clean washbasins   D. empty waste receptacles

25. To eliminate the cause of odors in toilet rooms, the tile floor should be mopped with   25.____

    A. a mild solution of soap and trisodium phosphate in water
    B. dilute lye solution followed by a hot water rinse
    C. dilute muriatic acid dissolved in hot water
    D. carbon tetrachloride dissolved in hot water

———

KEY (CORRECT ANSWERS)

1.	D		11.	B
2.	B		12.	D
3.	C		13.	A
4.	B		14.	C
5.	D		15.	B
6.	C		16.	D
7.	A		17.	A
8.	C		18.	B
9.	D		19.	D
10.	D		20.	C

21.	C
22.	D
23.	B
24.	D
25.	A

———

TEST 3

DIRECTIONS: Each question or incomplete statement is followed by several suggested answers or completions. Select the one that BEST answers the question or completes the statement. PRINT THE LETTER OF THE CORRECT ANSWER IN THE SPACE AT THE RIGHT.

1. The one of the following cleaning agents that should be used to remove an accumulation of grease from a concrete driveway is a(n)

   A. acid cleaner
   B. alkaline cleaner
   C. liquid soap
   D. solvent cleaner

   1._____

2. Of the following, the cleaning assignment which you would LEAST prefer to have performed *during* school hours is

   A. sweeping of corridors and stairs
   B. cleaning and polishing brass fixtures
   C. cleaning toilets
   D. dusting of offices, halls, and special rooms

   2._____

3. Specifications concerning window cleaners' anchors and safety belts must be in compliance with the rules and regulations outlined in the

   A. State Labor Law and Board of standards and Appeals
   B. Building Code
   C. Fire Department safety manual
   D. National Protection Association

   3._____

4. The difficulty of cleaning soil from surfaces is LEAST affected by the

   A. length of time between cleanings
   B. chemical nature of the soil
   C. smoothness of the surface being cleaned
   D. standard time allotted to the job

   4._____

5. The one of the following chemicals that a custodian should tell a cleaner to use to remove mildew from terrazzo is

   A. ammonia
   B. oxalic acid
   C. sodium hypochlorite
   D. sodium silicate

   5._____

6. Of the following, the one which is NOT a purpose of a cleaning Job breakdown is to

   A. eliminate unnecessary steps
   B. determine the type of floor wax to use
   C. rearrange the sequence of operations to save time
   D. combine steps or actions where practicable

   6._____

7. The BEST time of day to dust classroom furniture and woodwork is

   A. in the morning before the students arrive
   B. during the morning recess
   C. during the students' lunch time
   D. immediately after the students are dismissed for the day

   7._____

8. In order to clean an office with 20,000 aquare feet of space in four hours, using a standard of 900 square feet per hour, the number of cleaners you should assign to do the job is MOST NEARLY   8.____

    A. 4   B. 6   C. 8   D. 10

9. The area of a floor 35' wide and 45' long is, in square yards, most nearly   9.____

    A. 175   B. 262   C. 525   D. 1575

10. One of the important benefits to floors that wax does NOT provide is   10.____

    A. easier soil removal   B. improved stain resistance
    C. reduction in wear   D. resistance to fire

11. Domestic hot water storage reservoirs should be thoroughly cleand once   11.____

    A. a week   B. a month
    C. a year   D. every two years

Questions 12-14.

DIRECTIONS: Questions 12 through 14 are to be answered on the basis of the following passage.

The method of cleaning which should generally be used is the space assignment method. Under this method, the buildings to be cleaned are divided into different sections. Within each section, each crew of cleaners is assigned to do one particular cleaning job. For example, within a section, one crew may be assigned to cleaning offices, another to scrubbing floors, a third to collectign trash, and so on. Other methods which may be used are the post assignment method, and the gang cleaning method. Under the post assignment method, a cleaner is assigned to one area of a building and performs all cleaning jobs in that area. This method is seldom used except where buildings are so small and distant from each other that it is not economical to use the space assignment method. Under the gang cleaning method, a custodian takes a number of cleaners through a section of the building. These cleaners work as a group and complete the various cleaning jobs as they go. This metyod is generally used only where the building contains very larg open areas.

12. According to the above passage, under the space assignment method, each crew GENERALLY   12.____

    A. works as a group and does a variety of different cleaning jobs
    B. is assigned to one area and performs all cleaning jobs in that area
    C. does one particular cleaning job within a section of a building
    D. follows the custodian through a building containing large, open areas

13. According to the above passage, the post assignment method is used MOSTLY where the building to be cleaned are _____ in size and situated _____.   13.____

    A. large; close together   B. small; close together
    C. large; far apart   D. small; far apart

14. As used in the above passage, the word *economical* means MOST NEARLY   14.____

    A. thrifty   B. agreed   C. unusual   D. wasteful

15. New copper flashing that has been soldered should be cleaned with 15.____

    A. muriatic acid   B. plain water
    C. benzine   D. washing soda or lye

16. To improve the appearance and preserve a rubber tile floor, the BEST substance to use is 16.____

    A. wax   B. floor seal varnish
    C. plastic floor finish   D. none of the above

17. When waxing asphalt tile floors, the wax should be applied in several thin coats because 17.____

    A. one thick coat takes longer to apply
    B. it will dry faster and harder
    C. It is a more economical method
    D. the pores of the tile will be able to absorb the wax more readily

18. The floors of modern indoor swimming pools are USUALLY cleaned of sediment by means of 18.____

    A. long-handled wire brushes
    B. vacuum cleaning equipment
    C. water-resistant fiber brushes
    D. compressed air wall brush

19. A good disinfectant is one that will 19.____

    A. have a clean odor which will cover up disagreeable odors
    B. destroy germs and create more sanitary condition
    C. dissolve enerusted dirt and otyer sources of disagrreable odors
    D. dissolve grease and other materials that may cause stoppages in toilet waste lines

20. The surfaces of water coolers and door kick plates are cleaned BEST by using a cleaning solution and a 20.____

    A. brush   B. wet cloth
    C. cellulose sponge   D. wab of paper

21. When the diaphragm or bellows of a thermostatic radiator trap is found to be dirty. It is USUALLY cleaned with 21.____

    A. turpentine   B. carbon tetrachloride
    C. kerosene   D. mild soap and water

22. In general, the MOST efficient method for doing a cleaning Job is the method which 22.____

    A. must be repeated most frequently
    B. has the most different steps and operations
    C. gives the best results for the least amount of effort
    D. requires the efforts of the greatest number of cleaners

23. Chloride of lime should be used for the removal of

    A. alkali stains on wood
    B. grass stains on wood or marble
    C. indelible pencil and marking ink stains on concrete or terrazzo
    D. ink stains on wood

23.____

24. The one of the following that is a concrete floor sealer is

    A. sodium silicate   B. neatsfoot oil
    C. sodium hydroxide   D. linseed oil

24.____

25. The MAIN reason for applying floor finish to a floor surface is to

    A. protect against germs   B. protect the floor surface
    C. increase traction   D. waterproof the floor

25.____

KEY (CORRECT ANSWERS)

1.	D		11.	C
2.	C		12.	C
3.	A		13.	D
4.	D		14.	A
5.	C		15.	D
6.	B		16.	A
7.	A		17.	B
8.	B		18.	B
9.	A		19.	B
10.	D		20.	C

21.	C
22.	C
23.	C
24.	A
25.	B

EXAMINATION SECTION
TEST 1

DIRECTIONS: Each question or Incomplete statement is followed by several suggested answers or completions. Select the one that BEST answers the question or completes the statement. *PRINT THE LETTER OF THE CORRECT ANSWER IN THE SPACE AT THE RIGHT.*

1. Elevator cleaning is BEST done between   1.____

    A. 8 A.M. and 9 A.M.   B. 9 A.M. and 10 A.M.
    C. 12 Noon and 1 P.M.   D. 2:30 P.M. and 3:30 P.M.

2. The wax solution that is put on floors of elevators once a week is made of _____ part(s)   2.____
wax and _____ part(s) water.

    A. 1; 1   B. 1; 2   C. 2; 1   D. 3; 2

3. The cleaning of an elevator cab should take APPROXIMATELY   3.____

    A. 15 minutes
    B. 40 minutes
    C. one hour for every 225 square feet
    D. one hour for every 300 square feet

4. In washing windows, the blade of the squeegee should ALWAYS be   4.____

    A. dried after each stroke
    B. held straight against the glass
    C. used with as much water as possible
    D. wet after each stroke

5. Cleaners are instructed to leave a 4-inch space between the material in an incinerator   5.____
can and the top of the can.
This Is done MAINLY to

    A. follow sanitation department rules
    B. make it possible to pile cans on top of each other
    C. make the can easier to lift
    D. prevent spilling over of the material

6. A new corn broom should be soaked overnight before using it for the first time.   6.____
This is done to

    A. help the broom to keep its shape
    B. make it possible to use the broom for scrubbing
    C. make the broom wear evenly
    D. remove the brittleness of the broom's straws

7. After each day's use of the mop tank, the   7.____

    A. compartments and wringer should be rinsed and wiped dry
    B. compartments should be half-filled with clean water
    C. mop wringer should be left In the unreleased position
    D. wheels should be oiled and the excess oil wiped off

8. Elevator cab walls should be cleaned with a solution of water and   8.____

    A. ammonia   B. carbon tetraehloride
    C. kerosene   D. oil

9. Badly soiled ivory piano keys can BEST be cleaned by using   9.____

    A. trisodlum phosphate   B. kerosene
    C. alcohol on a clean rag   D. a feather duster

10. Which cleaning agent would be MOST harmful to a terrazzo floor?   10.____

    A. Trisodlum phosphate   B. Oil soap
    C. Powdered soap   D. Ammonia

11. Canvas window cleaning belts are BEST stored   11.____

    A. in the sink closet
    B. in the custodial storeroom
    C. hanging vertically by the buckle
    D. flat on a shelf In the workshop

Questions 12-15.

DIRECTIONS: Questions 12 through 15 are to be answered SOLELY on the basis of the information given in the following passage.

ACCIDENT PREVENTION

Many accidents and injuries can be prevented if employees learn to be more careful. The wearing of shoes with thin or badly worn soles or open toes can easily lead to foot injuries from tacks, nails, and chair and desk legs. Loose or torn clothing should not be worn near moving machinery. This is especially true of neckties which can very easily become caught in the machine. You should not place objects so that they block or partly block hallways, corridors, or other passageways. Even when they are stored in the proper place, tools, supplies, and equipment should be carefully placed or piled so as not to fall, nor have anything stick out from a pile. Before cabinets, lockers or ladders are moved, the tops should be cleared of anything which might injure someone or fall off. If necessary, use a dolly to move these or other bulky objects.

Despite all efforts to avoid accidents and injuries, however, some will happen. If an employee is injured, no matter how small the injury, he should report it to his supervisor and have the injury treated. A small cut that is not attended to can easily become infected and can cause more trouble than some injuries which at first seem more serious. It never pays to take chances.

12. According to the above passage, the one statement that is NOT true is that   12.____

    A. by being more careful, employees can reduce the number of accidents that happen
    B. women should wear shoes with open toes for comfort when working
    C. supplies should be piled so that nothing is sticking out from the pile
    D. if an employee sprains his wrist at work, he should tell his supervisor about it

13. According to the above passage, you should NOT wear loose clothing when you are   13.____

    A. in a corridor
    B. storing tools
    C. opening cabinets
    D. near moving machinery

14. According to the above passage, before moving a ladder, you should   14.____

    A. test all the rungs
    B. get a dolly to carry the ladder at all times
    C. remove everything from the top of the ladder which might fall off
    D. remove your necktie

15. According to the above passage, an employee who gets a slight cut should   15.____

    A. have it treated to help prevent infection
    B. know that a slight cut becomes more easily Infected than a big cut
    C. pay no attention to it as it can't become serious
    D. realize that it is more serious than any other type of injury

16. The word *abrasive* means MOST NEARLY the same as   16.____

    A. smooth
    B. powdered
    C. scratchy
    D. sticky

17. Oxalic acid can be used to   17.____

    A. remove ink spots from wood
    B. clear floor drains
    C. solder copper flashing
    D. polish brass

18. The BEST material for sealing a terrazzo floor is   18.____

    A. varnish
    B. a penetrating seal
    C. shellac
    D. a surface seal

19. The MOST troublesome feature in cleaning public washrooms is   19.____

    A. cleaning and deodorizing the urinals
    B. washing the toilet bowls
    C. mopping the tile floors
    D. removing chewing gum from the floors

20. In order to improve its appearance, extend its life, and reduce the labor involved in dusting, wood furniture should be polished with   20.____

    A. an oil polish
    B. a water emulsion wax
    C. a silicone and spirit chemical spray
    D. clear water

21. Of the following, the LARGEST individual item of expense in operating a public building is generally the cost of   21.____

    A. cleaning
    B. heating fuel
    C. electricity
    D. elevator service

22. The CHIEF purpose for changing the handle of a floor brush from one side of the brush block to the other side is to

    A. allow the cleaner to change hands
    B. make both sides of the brush equally dirty
    C. give both sides of the brush equal wear
    D. change the angle of sweeping

22.____

23. Of the following, the weight of mop MOST likely used in the nightly mopping of corridors, halls, or lobbies is _____ ounces.

    A. 8   B. 16   C. 24   D. 50

23.____

24. After a sweeping assignment is completed, floor brushes should be stored

    A. in a pan of water
    B. by hanging the brushes on pegs or nails
    C. by piling the brushes on each other carefully
    D. in a normal sweeping position, bristles resting on the floor

24.____

25. Nylon treated scrubbing discs

    A. require more water than scrubbing brushes
    B. require more detergent solution than scrubbing brushes
    C. must be used with cold water only
    D. are generally more effective than steel wool pads

25.____

KEY(CORRECT ANSWERS)

1.	B		11.	C
2.	C		12.	B
3.	A		13.	D
4.	A		14.	C
5.	D		15.	A
6.	D		16.	C
7.	A		17.	A
8.	A		18.	B
9.	C		19.	A
10.	A		20.	C

21.	A
22.	C
23.	C
24.	B
25.	D

TEST 2

DIRECTIONS: Each question or incomplete statement is followed by several suggested answers or completions. Select the one that BEST answers the question or completes the statement. *PRINT THE LETTER OF THE CORRECT ANSWER IN THE SPACE AT THE RIGHT.*

1. The BEST agent to use to remove chewing gum from fabric is   1.____

    A. ammonia   B. chlorine bleach
    C. a degreaser   D. water

2. Water emulsion wax should NOT be used on   2.____

    A. linoleum   B. cork tile flooring
    C. furniture   D. rubber tile flooring

3. Tops of desks, file cabinets, and bookcases are BEST dusted with a   3.____

    A. damp cloth   B. treated cotton cloth
    C. damp sponge   D. feather duster

4. The one of the following which is NOT a material in scrub brushes is   4.____

    A. tampico   B. terrazzo   C. palmetto   D. bassine

5. A chamois is PROPERLY used to   5.____

    A. wash enamel surfaces   B. wash window glass
    C. dry enamel surfaces   D. dry window glass

6. The PROPER sequence of operations used in cleaning an office, when the floor is to be   6.____
   swept with a broom is

    A. clean ashtrays, empty wastebaskets, sweep, dust
    B. sweep, dust, clean ashtrays, empty wastebaskets
    C. dust, sweep, clean ashtrays, empty wastebaskets
    D. clean ashtrays, empty wastebaskets, dust, sweep

7. A paper sticker should be used by a cleaner to   7.____

    A. pick up litter and fruit skins
    B. make temporary warning signs to be placed around wet floor areas
    C. indicate on the elevator panel on which floor he is working
    D. feed old newspapers into the Incinerator

8. The type of floor which should be cleaned by sweeping then mopping with an abrasive   8.____
   detergent is the _____ floor.

    A. painted cement   B. unpainted cement
    C. asphalt tile   D. terrazzo

9. The term *cutting the water* refers to one step in the procedure for   9.____

    A. cleaning windows   B. treating boiler water
    C. watering lawns   D. washing walls

10. Stains on ceramic tile may be removed by very carefully using a dilute solution of _____   10.____
    acid.

    A. acetic   B. oxalic
    C. sulphuric   D. hydrochloric

11. The directions on the label of a bottle of detergent call for mixing four ounces of deter-   11.____
    gent with one gallon of water to make a cleaning solution for washing floors.
    In order to obtain a LARGER amount of solution of the same strength, one quart of the
    detergent should be mixed with _____ gallons of water.

    A. 2   B. 4   C. 6   D. 8

12. Of the following materials, the one that should be used to produce the MOST resilient   12.____
    flooring is

    A. concrete   B. terrazzo
    C. ceramic tile   D. asphalt tile

13. Sweeping compound is used on concrete floors MAINLY to   13.____

    A. keep the dust down
    B. polish the floor
    C. harden the floor surface
    D. indicate which part of the floor has not been swept

14. The type of floor finish or wax that will produce an anti-slip surface on resilient floor cov-   14.____
    erings is

    A. resin-based floor finish
    B. water emulsion wax
    C. paste wax
    D. paraffin

15. High sheen and good wearing qualities can be obtained when polishing a waxed floor by   15.____
    using an electric scrubbing machine equipped with

    A. nylon disks   B. soft brushes
    C. steel wool pads   D. pumice wheels

16. Spalling of the surface of a marble floor may result if the floor is washed with   16.____

    A. a solution of trisodium phosphate
    B. a soft soap solution
    C. a neutral liquid detergent solution
    D. cold water

Questions 17-20.

DIRECTIONS: Column I lists cleaning agents used by a custodian. Cleaning operations are given in Column II. Select the MOST common cleaning operation for the cleaning agents listed in Column I and print the letter representing your choice in the space at the right.

COLUMN I	COLUMN II	
17. Ammonia	A. Add water to cleanmarble walls	17._____
18. Muriatic acid	B. Remove chewing gum from wood floors	18._____
19. Carbon tetrachloride	C. Wash down calcimined ceilings	19._____
20. Trisodium phosphate	D. Add to water for washing rubber tile	20._____
	E. Remove stains from porcelain	

Questions 21-24.

DIRECTIONS: Questions 21 through 24 are to be answered SOLELY on the basis of the following paragraph.

There are on the market many cleaning agents for which amazing claims are made. Chemical analysis shows that the majority of them are well-known chemicals slightly modified and packaged and sold under various trade names. For that reason, the agents which have been selected for your use are those whose cleaning properties are well-known and whose use can be standardized. It is obviously undesirable to offer too wide a selection as that would be confusing to the cleaner, but a sufficient number must be provided so that a satisfactory agent is available for each task.

21. According to the above paragraph,   21._____

    A. there are few cleaning agents on the market
    B. there are no really good cleaning agents on the market
    C. cleaning agents are sold under several different brand names
    D. all cleaning agents are the same

22. According to the above paragraph,   22._____

    A. all cleaning agents should be chemically analyzed before use
    B. the best cleaning agents are those for which no claims are made by the manufacturer
    C. different cleaning agents may be needed for different tasks
    D. all cleaning agents have been standardized by the federal government

57

23. As used in the above paragraph, the word *amazing* means   23.____

    A. illegal   B. untrue
    C. astonishing   D. specific

24. As used in the above paragraph, the word *modified* means   24.____

    A. changed   B. refined
    C. labelled   D. diluted

25. The one of the following which can be used BOTH as a disinfectant and as a bleach is   25.____

    A. chlorine solution   B. powdered whiting
    C. pine oil   D. boric acid

KEY(CORRECT ANSWERS)

1.	C	11.	D
2.	C	12.	D
3.	B	13.	A
4.	B	14.	A
5.	D	15.	B
6.	A	16.	A
7.	A	17.	A
8.	B	18.	E
9.	A	19.	B
10.	D	20.	D

21.	C
22.	C
23.	C
24.	A
25.	A

TEST 3

DIRECTIONS: Each question or incomplete statement is followed by several suggested answers or completions. Select the one that BEST answers the question or completes the statement. *PRINT THE LETTER OF THE CORRECT ANSWER IN THE SPACE AT THE RIGHT.*

1. Which one of the following is the BEST procedure to follow when the linoleum floor of a meeting room containing movable furniture is to be mopped?   1.____

    A. The furniture should be moved by sliding it along the floor to prevent Injury to the cleaners.
    B. The furniture should not be moved.
    C. The furniture should be moved by lifting it and carrying it to a clear spot to prevent damage to the linoleum.
    D. Very little water should be used in order to prevent the legs of the furniture from getting wet.

2. Asphalt tile flooring that has been subjected to oily compounds   2.____

    A. may last indefinitely
    B. must be removed and replaced with new asphalt tile immediately
    C. may be restored to hardness and lustre by several moppings with hot water and several applications of water wax
    D. must be restored to original condition by several moppings with kerosene

3. The use of alcohol in water for washing windows is NOT recommended because it   3.____

    A. is a hazard to the cleaner in that he may be affected by the fumes
    B. will damage the paint around the edges of the glass
    C. pits the surface of the glass
    D. destroys the bristles of the brush applying the solution to the pane

4. Of the following, the BEST material to use for removing grass stains on marble or wood is   4.____

    A. oxalic acid   B. chloride of lime
    C. sodium silicate   D. sodium hypochlorite

5. Shades or Venetian blinds are PREFERABLY cleaned with a   5.____

    A. feather duster   B. counter brush
    C. damp sponge   D. vacuum cleaner

6. Plated metal surfaces which are protected by a thin coat of clear lacquer should be cleaned with a(n)   6.____

    A. abrasive compound   B. liquid polish
    C. mild soap solution   D. lemon oil solution

7. Wet mop filler replacements are ordered by   7.____

    A. length   B. weight
    C. number of strands   D. trade number

8. The BEST way to determine the value of a cleaning material is by   8._____

    A. performance testing
    B. manufacturer's literature
    C. written specifications
    D. interviews with manufacturer's salesmen

9. The instructions on a container of cleaning compound states: *Mix one pound of compound in 5 gallons of water.* Using these instructions, the amount of compound which should be added to 15 quarts of water is MOST likely _____ ounces.   9._____

    A. 3   B. 8   C. 12   D. 48

10. In lifting a heavy can, a cleaner should keep his   10._____

    A. back and knees straight
    B. back bent and knees straight
    C. knees and back bent
    D. knees bent and back straight

11. If a man is injured on the Job and it is likely that he has broken bones, the foreman should   11._____

    A. call for an ambulance
    B. call the superintendent
    C. take him to the hospital in his car
    D. tell the injured man to go to the hospital immediately

12. The MAIN reason for not letting dust cloths or oily rags pile up in storage closets is that   12._____

    A. a fire may start from this material
    B. the closet will not look neat and orderly
    C. the oil may soak into the floor and stain it
    D. they take up valuable space which may be put to better uses

13. Suppose, in making your rounds, you come upon a small oil and grease fire in a basement. After putting in a fire alarm, you find the fire extinguisher is out of order. The BEST thing for you to do is to   13._____

    A. do nothing since you have put in an alarm
    B. open all the doors and windows
    C. throw earth and sand on the fire
    D. throw water on the fire

14. The BEST thing to do for a man who feels he is about to faint is to   14._____

    A. apply a cold compress to his forehead
    B. give him some cold water to drink
    C. lower his head between his knees
    D. move him out to the fresh air

15. In removing the end of a broken bulb from a socket, the cleaner should stick a hard rub-   15._____
ber wedge into the socket and

    A. pull the wedge down
    B. push the wedge up
    C. turn the wedge to the right
    D. turn the wedge to the left

16. To keep chrome-plated metal clean, you should   16._____

    A. polish with fine steel wool
    B. wash with soapy water and polish with soft cloth
    C. clean with scouring powder and polish with soft cloth
    D. none of the above

17. After wetting down the floor with water solution, the BEST mop to use is   17._____

    A. a mop wet with clean water
    B. one wrung out in solution water
    C. a dry mop
    D. one wrung out in clear water

18. After sweeping and dusting a room, the LAST thing that should be done is   18._____

    A. empty wastebasket   B. switch off lights
    C. close windows   D. clean the furniture

19. Before repainting becomes necessary, a painted wall can USUALLY be washed com-   19._____
pletely

    A. only once   B. two or three times
    C. eight to ten times   D. sixteen to twenty times

20. The FIRST step In routine cleaning of offices at night should be   20._____

    A. sweeping floors   B. emptying ashtrays
    C. dusting furniture   D. damp mopping the floors

21. Among the factors pertaining to the maintenance and cleaning of a building, the one   21._____
MOST likely to be under the control of the building custodian is the

    A. size of the area
    B. density of occupancy
    C. type of occupancy
    D. standards to be maintained

22. *Treated or dustless* sweeping of resilient-type floors requires   22._____

    A. spraying the floors with water to keep the dust down
    B. spreading sweeping compound on the floor
    C. sweeping cloths that are chemically treated with mineral oil
    D. spraying the sweeping tool with neatsfoot oil

23. A modern central vacuum cleaner system   23._____

    A. is cheaper to operate than one portable machine
    B. generally produces less suction than a portable machine
    C. conveys the dirt directly to a basement tank
    D. must be operated only in the daytime

24. Disinfectants are used in cleaning solutions for toilet rooms MAINLY to

    A. cover up unpleasant odors
    B. destroy some harmful bacteria
    C. dissolve encrusted dirt
    D. reduce need for frequent cleaning

24.____

25. If chrome-plated fittings become greasy, they should be cleaned with

    A. scouring powder
    C. kerosene

    B. weak vinegar solution
    D. gasoline

25.____

_____

KEY(CORRECT ANSWERS)

1.	C	11.	A
2.	C	12.	A
3.	B	13.	C
4.	D	14.	C
5.	D	15.	D
6.	C	16.	B
7.	B	17.	C
8.	A	18.	B
9.	C	19.	B
10.	D	20.	B

21.	D
22.	C
23.	C
24.	B
25.	C

_____

DIRECTIONS: Each question or incomplete statement is followed by several suggested answers or completions. Select the one that BEST answers the question or completes the Statement. *PRINT THE LETTER OF THE CORRECT ANSWER IN THE SPACE AT THE RIGHT.*

1. Which of the following substances causes asphalt tile to turn spongy?   1.____

    A. Oil   B. Varnish   C. Water   D. Dust

2. Which of the following would NOT cause asphalt tile to turn yellow?   2.____

    A. A layer of dust   B. Varnish
    C. Lacquer   D. Water

3. Which one of the following is LEAST likely to be an advantage of waxing a floor?   3.____

    A. Helps to make a room quieter
    B. Helps to reduce wear on the floor
    C. Gives a pleasant shine to the floor
    D. Improves the stain resistance of the floor

4. The action of liquid cleaner on a floor with built-up wax is to   4.____

    A. make the wax disappear into the air
    B. turn the wax into little grains that must be swept up in a vacuum cleaner
    C. soften the wax, which has to be scrubbed away and then rinsed off
    D. make the floor waterproof

5. After how many waxings should built-up wax be removed from a floor?   5.____
Every

    A. waxing   B. 3 waxings   C. 6 waxings   D. 12 waxings

6. Manuals on floor cleaning describe methods of cleaning *resilient flooring.*   6.____
Which of the following kinds of flooring surfaces is NOT resilient?
_____ tile.

    A. Cork   B. Asphalt   C. Vinyl   D. Terrazzo

7. In buffing a floor, it is NOT desirable to use a polishing brush because the   7.____

    A. brush will scratch the surface you are trying to polish
    B. strands of the brush fall out easily
    C. brush is often used for other purposes
    D. brush does not usually remove deep scuff marks

8. *Rolling* results when only the upper parts of a wax coat dry, leaving the lower parts wet.   8.____
In waxing a floor, this condition comes from

    A. putting on too thick a coat of wax
    B. putting on too thin a coat of wax
    C. rinsing the floor before applying the wax
    D. leaving soap on the floor before applying the wax

9. After a cork or linoleum floor is installed, how long should you wait before you mop the floor for the FIRST time?   9._____

    A. 1 days   B. 3 days   C. 12 hours   D. 2 weeks

10. On sweeping stairways, you should direct your men to make a practice of sweeping them   10._____

    A. when traffic is heavy so that people can see them working
    B. whenever they have free time during the day
    C. during the morning at a time when traffic is lightest
    D. in the middle of the day when the traffic is medium heavy

11. How often must public corridors be swept?   11._____

    A. Only when a visible amount of dirt piles up
    B. Every day
    C. Once a week
    D. Every three days

12. You should NOT use an oily mop to sweep floor because it   12._____

    A. leaves a sticky film that can catch dust
    B. eats away at the floor like acid
    C. makes the floor completely waterproof
    D. prevents wax from being applied

13. Which of the following would NOT be used on a concrete floor?   13._____

    A. Water base wax   B. Oily sweeping compound
    C. Solvent wax   D. Wire brush

14. You should NOT use an alkaline cleaner on linoleum floors because the cleaner   14._____

    A. will make the floor shine too brightly
    B. makes the linoleum sticky
    C. makes the linoleum crack and curl
    D. costs too much to be practical

15. The BEST way of wet mopping a large floor area is to mop the floor area   15._____

    A. with a circular motion
    B. from side to side or with a figure eight motion
    C. with forward and back strokes
    D. alternate side to side forward and back

16. The type of product to use when cleaning terrazzo floors is   16._____

    A. mild cleaner   B. diluted acid solution
    C. scouring powder   D. paste wax

17. A cleaner was wet mopping an asphalt tile floor. He decided to make the floor as wet as   17.____
possible.
For him to do this is a

    A. *good* idea, because the more water you use, the cleaner the floor will be
    B. *bad* idea, because water should never be wasted
    C. *good* idea, because the floor will not have to be washed as often
    D. *bad* idea, because the excess water will eventually damage the floor surface

18. When you wet clean a stairway by hand, you need two buckets.   18.____
One of them is for the cleaning solution, and the other one is used for

    A. extra ammonia for cleaning
    B. rinsing, and should be filled with clean water
    C. putting out fires, and should be filled with sand
    D. storage of equipment

19. The cleaning of stairways is USUALLY scheduled to be done with   19.____

    A. corridor cleaning   B. sidewalk cleaning
    C. incinerator work   D. move-outs

20. *Dry cleaning* in relation to a building refers to   20.____

    A. a reconditioning process that restores the appearance of a floor and protects the surface by buffing
    B. dusting of a wall area with specially treated cloth in order to produce a sheen
    C. patch waxing of a floor with a powdered wax compound
    D. dry mopping only of a floor area

Questions 21-24.

DIRECTION: Questions 21 through 24, inclusive, are to be answered SOLELY on the basis of the following paragraph.

All cleaning agents and supplies should be kept in a central storeroom which should be kept locked and only the custodian, store keeper, and foreman should have keys. Shelving should be provided for the smaller items, while barrels containing scouring powder or other bulk material should be set on the floor or on special cradles. Each compartment in the shelves should be marked plainly and only the item indicated stored therein. Each barrel should also be marked plainly. It may also be desirable to keep special items such as electric lamps, flashlight batteries, etc. in a locked cabinet or separate room to which only the custodian and the night building foreman have keys.

21. According to the above paragraph, scouring powder   21.____

    A. should be kept on shelves
    B. comes in one-pound cans
    C. should be kept in a locked cabinet
    D. is a bulk material

22. According to the above paragraph, 22.____

    A. the storekeeper should not be entrusted with the safekeeping of lightbulbs
    B. flashlight batteries should be stored in barrels
    C. the central storeroom should be kept locked
    D. only special items should be stored under lock and key

23. According to the above paragraph, 23.____

    A. each shelf compartment should contain at least four different Items
    B. barrels must be stored in cradles
    C. all items stored should be in marked compartments
    D. crates of lightbulbs should be stored in cradles

24. As used In the above paragraph, the word *cradle* means a 24.____

    A. dolly   B. support
    C. doll's bed   D. hand truck

25. The material recommended for removing blood or fruit stains from concrete is 25.____

    A. soft soap   B. neatsfoot oil
    C. oxalic acid   D. ammonia

KEY (CORRECT ANSWER)

1.	A		11.	B
2.	A		12.	A
3.	A		13.	B
4.	C		14.	C
5.	C		15.	B
6.	D		16.	A
7.	D		17.	D
8.	A		18.	B
9.	B		19.	A
10.	C		20.	A

21. D
22. C
23. C
24. B
25. D

TEST 2

DIRECTIONS: Each question or incomplete statement Is followed by several suggested answers or completions. Select the one that BEST answers the question or completes the statement. *PRINT THE LETTER OF THE CORRECT ANSWER IN THE SPACE AT THE RIGHT.*

1. The wall surface which does NOT have to be washed from the bottom up to avoid streak-ing is a(n) _____ wall.

    A. semi-gloss painted   B. enamel painted
    C. glazed tile   D. unglazed tile

1.____

2. The one of the following practices which is GENERALLY recommended to prolong the useful life of a corn broom is

    A. soaking a new broom overnight before using it for the first time to remove brittle-ness
    B. storing the broom with the tips of the straws resting on the floor to keep the edges even
    C. keeping the straws moistened when sweeping
    D. storing the broom in a warm humid enclosure to prevent drying of the bristles

2.____

3. While a cleaner is sweeping the public corridors and stairways, he notices some crayon marks on walls and stains on the floors.
He should

    A. stop sweeping and remove the stains immediately
    B. finish sweeping and then return to remove the stains
    C. make note of the marks and stains in his building and remove them once a month
    D. make a note of the marks and stains and report them to the superintendent so that the cause can be eliminated before the stains are removed

3.____

4. When transporting the equipment required for mopping stairhalls and corridors, a cleaner should NOT

    A. attempt to do it alone
    B. carry water in the pails because spillage may cause a tenant to slip and fall
    C. use the elevator
    D. carry the equipment in both hands when climbing stairs

4.____

5. A cleaner should apply washing solution to a portion of a painted wall and should rinse the same area before applying the solution to another area.
In order to allow sufficient time for the solution to take effect on the soil, the area cov-ered each time should be APPROXIMATELY _____ square feet.

    A. 20   B. 60   C. 160   D. 600

5.____

6. Asphalt tile floors should be maintained by coating them with

    A. water emulsion wax   B. paste wax
    C. oil emulsion wax   D. neatsfoot oil

6.____

7. The broom with which a cleaner should sweep an asphalt-paved playground is the _____ broom.

   A. hair   B. corn   C. garage   D. Scotch

7.___

8. The central vacuum cleaning system should be cleaned

   A. weekly   B. twice weekly
   C. daily   D. when necessary

8.___

9. The FIRST thing a window cleaner should do is

   A. test window bolts
   B. see that cleaning tools are good
   C. cheak window belt
   D. nit lean too heavily on glass

9.___

10. During a shortage of custodial help in a public building, the cleaning task which will probably receive LEAST attention is

   A. picking up sweepings   B. emptying ashtrays
   C. washing walls   D. dust-mopping offices

10.___

11. Of the following substances commonly used on floors, the MOST flammable is

   A. resin-based floor finish   B. floor sealer
   C. water emulsion wax   D. trisodium phosphate

11.___

12. The MOST effective method for cleaning badly soiled carpeting is

   A. wet shampooing   B. vacuum cleaning
   C. dry shampooing   D. wire brushing

12.___

13. Painted walls and ceilings should be brushed down

   A. daily
   B. weekly
   C. every month, especially during the winter
   D. two or three times a year

13.___

14. If an asphalt tile floor become excessively dirty, the method of cleaning should include

   A. the use of kerosene or benzine as a solvent
   B. the use of a solution of modified laundry soda
   C. sanding down the spotted areas with a sanding machine on the wet floor
   D. use of a light oil and treated mop

14.___

15. To remove light stains from marble walls, the BEST method is to

   A. use steel wool and a scouring powder, then rinse with clear warm water
   B. was the stained area with a dilute acid solution
   C. sand down the spot first, then wash with mild soap solution
   D. wet marble first, then scrub with mild soap solution using a soft fiber brush

15.___

16. To rid a toilet room of objectionable odors, the PROPER method is to   16._____

    A. spread some chloride of lime on the floor
    B. place deodorizer cubes in a box hung on the wall
    C. wash the floor with hot water containing a little kerosene
    D. wash the floor with hot water into which some disinfectant has been poured

17. Toilet rooms, to be cleaned properly, should be swept   17._____

    A. daily
    B. and mopped daily
    C. daily and mopped twice a week
    D. daily and mopped thoroughly at the end of the

18. In waxing a floor, it is usually BEST to   18._____

    A. start the waxing under stationary furniture and then do the aisles
    B. pour the wax on the floor, spreading it under the desks with a wax mop
    C. remove the old wax coat before rewaxing
    D. wet mop the floor after the second coat has dried to obtain a high polish

19. Of the following, the MOST important reason why a wet mop should NOT be wrung out   19._____
by hand is that

    A. the strings of the mop will be damaged by hand-wringing
    B. sharp objects picked up by the mop may injure the hands
    C. the mop cannot be made dry enough by hand-wringing
    D. fine dirt will become embedded in the strings of the mop

20. When a painted wall is washed by hand, the wall should be washed from the   20._____

    A. top down, with a soaking wet sponge
    B. bottom up, with a soaking wet sponge
    C. top down, with a damp sponge
    D. bottom up, with a damp sponge

21. When a painted wall is brushed with a clean lambswool duster, the duster should be   21._____
drawn _____ with a _____ pressure.

    A. downward; light   B. upward; light
    C. downward; firm   D. upward; firm

22. The one of the following terms which BEST describes the size of a floor brush is   22._____

    A. 72 cubic inch   B. 32 ounce
    C. 24 inch   D. 10 square foot

23. Terrazzo floors should be mopped periodically with a(n)   23._____

    A. acid solution
    B. neutral detergent in warm water
    C. mop treated with kerosene
    D. strong alkaline solution

24. The MAIN reason why the handle of a reversible floor brush should be shifted from one   24.____
     side of the brush block to the opposite side is to

    A. change the angle at which the brush sweeps the floor
    B. give equal wear to both sides of the brush
    C. permit the brush to sweep hard-to-reach areas
    D. make it easier to sweep backward

25. When a long corridor is swept with a floor brush, it is good practice to   25.____

    A. push the brush with moderately long strokes and flick it after each stroke
    B. press on the brush and push it the whole length of the corridor in one sweep
    C. pull the brush inward with short, brisk strokes
    D. sweep across rather than down the length of the corridor

---

KEY (CORRECT ANSWERS)

1.	C	11.	B
2.	A	12.	A
3.	B	13.	D
4.	D	14.	D
5.	C	15.	D
6.	A	16.	D
7.	C	17.	B
8.	B	18.	A
9.	C	19.	B
10.	C	20.	D

21.	A
22.	C
23.	B
24.	B
25.	A

TEST 3

DIRECTIONS: Each question or incomplete statement is followed by several suggested answers or completions. Select the one that BEST answers the question or completes the Statement. *PRINT THE LETTER OF THE CORRECT ANSWER IN THE SPACE AT THE RIGHT.*

1. The MOST common cause of slipperiness of a terrazzo floor after it has been washed is the

    A. failure to rinse the floor clean of the cleaning agent
    B. destruction of the floor seal by the cleaning agent
    C. incomplete removal of dirt from the floor
    D. use of oil in the cleaning process

1.____

2. When electric lighting fixtures are washed, a precaution that should be observed is:

    A. The metal part of the fixture should be washed with a warm mild ammonia solution
    B. Holding screws of the glass globe should be loosened about one-half turn after they have all been applied to the cleaned globe
    C. Trisodium phosphate should not be used in washing glass globes because it dulls the glass
    D. Chain links of the fixture should be loosened to enable removal of the entire fixture for cleaning

2.____

3. A cleaner will make the BEST impression on the office staff if he

    A. impresses them with the importance of his job
    B. says little and is cold and distant
    C. is easy-going and good-natured
    D. is courteous and performs his duties with as little delay as possible

3.____

4. If it is necessary to wash stairways, this should be done during the

    A. day   B. night
    C. weekend   D. morning rush hour

4.____

5. A detergent is GENERALLY used in

    A. waterproofing walls   B. killing crabgrass
    C. cleaning floor and walls   D. exterminating rodents

5.____

6. Many new products are used in new buildings for floors, walls, and other surfaces. A cleaner should determine the BEST procedure to be used to clean such new surfaces by

    A. referring to the manual of procedures
    B. obtaining information on the cleaning procedure from the manufacturer
    C. asking the advice of the mechanics who installed the new material
    D. asking the district supervisor how to clean the surfaces

6.____

7. A window cleaner should carefully examine his safety belt

    A. once a week
    B. before he puts it on each time
    C. once a month
    D. once before he enters a building

7.____

8. One of your cleaners was injured as a result of slipping on an oily floor. This type of accident is MOST likely due to

    A. defective equipment
    B. the physical condition of the cleaner
    C. failure to use proper safety appliances
    D. poor housekeeping

8.____

9. For wet mopping the floor of a corridor by hand, the MINIMUM number of pails needed is

    A. one   B. two   C. three   D. four

9.____

10. A comparison of wet mopping by hand with scrubbing by hand indicates that mopping

    A. needs more cleaning solution
    B. is more time-consuming
    C. requires twice as much water
    D. is less effective on hardened soil

10.____

11. Chrome fixtures should be cleaned by

    A. using a mild soap solution then polishing with a soft cloth
    B. dusting lightly, then wax with an oil base wax
    C. polishing with a scouring pad
    D. washing with a solution of water and ammonia, then rinsing with a detergent

11.____

12. The BEST way for a building custodian to tell if the night cleaners have done their work well is to check

    A. on how much cleaning material has been used
    B. on how much wastepaper was collected
    C. the building for cleanliness
    D. the floor mops to see if they are still wet

12.____

13. THe one of the following items which ordinarily requires the MOST time to wash is a(n)

    A. 5 ft x 10 ft. Venetian blind
    B. 4 ft fluorescent fixture
    C. incandescent fixture
    D. 5 ft x 10 ft ceramic tile floor

13.____

14. A broom that has been properly used should GENERALLY be replaced after

    A. it has been used for one month
    B. its bristles have been worn down by more than one-third of their original length
    C. it has been used for two months
    D. its bristles have been worn down by more than two-thirds of their original length

14.____

15. Carbon tetrachloride is NOT recommended for cleaning purposes because of

    A. the poisonous nature of its fumes
    B. its limited cleaning value
    C. the damaging effects it has on equipment
    D. the difficulty of application

15.____

16. Proper care of floor brushes includes 16.____

    A. washing brushes daily after each use with warm soap solution
    B. dipping brushes in kerosene periodically to remove dirt
    C. washing with warm soap solution at least once a month
    D. avoiding contact with soap or soda solutions to prevent drying of bristles

17. Of the following, the cleaning assignment which you would LEAST prefer to have per- 17.____
formed during school hours is

    A. sweeping of corridors and stairs
    B. cleaning and polishing of brass fixtures
    C. cleaning toilets
    D. dusting of offices, halls, and special rooms

18. A cleaning detergent is composed of 18.____

    A. cleaning acids   B. salts
    C. sodium compounds   D. alkaline compounds

19. Neatsfoot oil is commonly used to 19.____

    A. oil light machinery
    B. prepare sweeping compound
    C. clean metal fixtures
    D. treat leather-covered chairs

20. The one of the following terms which BEST describes the size of a floor mop is 20.____

    A. 10 quart   B. 32 ounce
    C. 24 inch O.D.   D. 10 square feet

21. Cleaners will USUALLY be motivated to do a good job by a custodian who 21.____

    A. lets them get away with poor performance
    B. treats them fairly
    C. treats some of them more favorably than others
    D. lets them take a nap in the afternoon

22. When changing brushes on a scrubbing machine, of the following, the FIRST step to 22.____
take is to

    A. lock the switch in the *off* position
    B. be sure the power cable electric plug supplying the machine is disconnected from
       the wall outlet
    C. place the machine on top of the positioned brushes
    D. dip the brushes in water

23. The BEST method or tool to use for cleaning dust from an unplastered cinderblock wall is 23.____

    A. a tampico brush with stock cleaning solution
    B. a vacuum cleaner
    C. water under pressure from hose and nozzle
    D. a feather duster

24. The BEST reason for cleaning lightbulbs is

    A. the bulb willlast longer
    B. removing dust
    C. obtaining optimum light
    D. preventing electrical shock

24.___

25. Effluorescence may BEST be removed from brickwork by washing with a solution of _____ acid.

    A. muriatic   B. citric   C. carbonic   D. nitric

25.___

KEY (CORRECT ANSWERS)

1.	A		11.	A
2.	B		12.	C
3.	D		13.	A
4.	C		14.	B
5.	C		15.	A
6.	B		16.	C
7.	B		17.	C
8.	D		18.	C
9.	B		19.	D
10.	D		20.	B

21.	B
22.	B
23.	B
24.	C
25.	A

EXAMINATION SECTION
TEST 1

DIRECTIONS: Each question or incomplete statement is followed by several suggested answers or completions. Select the one that BEST answers the question or completes the statement. *PRINT THE LETTER OF THE CORRECT ANSWER IN THE SPACE AT THE RIGHT.*

1. In the wintertime, the FIRST thing a custodian does in the morning, after throwing the main switch, is to

    A. take a reading of the electric meter
    B. prepare his daily report of fuel consumption
    C. prepare sweeping compound
    D. inspect the water gauge of his boilers

1.____

2. Rubbish, stones, sticks, and papers on lawns in front of school buildings are MOST effectively collected by means of a

    A. 30 inch floor brush with thickly set bristles
    B. corn broom
    C. 4 foot pole with a nail set in the bottom of it
    D. rake

2.____

3. Which of the following statements about sweeping is NOT correct?

    A. Corridors and stairs should not be swept during school hours.
    B. Classrooms should usually be swept daily after the close of the afternoon session.
    C. Dry sweeping is not to be used in classrooms or corridors.
    D. Special rooms, as sewing rooms, may be swept during school hours if unoccupied.

3.____

4. The PROPER size of floor brush to be used in classrooms with fixed seats is _____ inches.

    A. 36   B. 24   C. 16   D. 6

4.____

5. Sweeping compound made of oiled sawdust should NOT be used on _____ floors.

    A. cement   B. rubber tile
    C. oiled wood   D. composition

5.____

6. In oiling a wood floor, it is GOOD practice to

    A. apply the oil with a dipped mop up to the baseboards of the walls
    B. avoid application of oil closer than 6 inches of the baseboards
    C. keep the oil about one inch from the baseboard
    D. make sure that oil is applied to the floors under radiators

6.____

7. Of the following, the LEAST desirable agent for cleaning blackboards is

    A. damp cloth
    B. clear warm water applied with a sponge
    C. warm water with a little kerosene
    D. warm water containing a mild soap solution

7.____

8. Chalk trays of blackboards should be washed and cleaned   8.____

    A. once a week
    B. daily
    C. only when the teacher reports cleaning needed
    D. once a month

9. In cleaning rooms by means of a central vacuum cleaning system,   9.____

    A. sweeping compound is used merely to prevent dust from rising
    B. rooms need cleaning only twice a week because the machine takes up the oil
    C. wood floors must be oiled more frequently as the machine takes up the oil
    D. the cleaner should not press down upon the tool but should guide it across the floor

10. A gas leak is suspected in the home economics class of a school. The procedure in   10.____
    locating the leak is to

    A. use a lighted match
    B. use a safety lamp
    C. place nose close to line and smell each section
    D. use soapsuds

11. The MOST important reason for placing asbestos jackets on steam lines is to   11.____

    A. prevent persons from burning their hands
    B. prevent heat loss
    C. protect the lines from injury
    D. make the lines appear more presentable

12. If the flag is used on a speaker's platform, it should be displayed   12.____

    A. above and behind the speaker
    B. as a drape over the front of the platform
    C. as a rosette over the speaker's head
    D. as a cover over the speaker's desk

13. When the flag of the United States of America is displayed from a staff projecting from   13.____
    the front of the building, it should be

    A. extended to the tip of the staff
    B. extended to about one foot from the tip of the staff
    C. secured so that there is a sag in the line
    D. extended slowly to the tip of the staff and then drawn back rapidly about 15 inches

14. The common soda-acid fire extinguisher should be checked and refilled   14.____

    A. every week   B. every month
    C. once a year   D. only if used

15. A small fire has broken out in an electric motor in a sump pump. The lubricant has appar-   15.____
    ently caught fire. The PROPER extinguisher to use is

    A. sand
    B. carbon tetrachloride (pyrene) fire extinguisher

C. soda-acid fire extinguisher
D. water under pressure from a hose

16. While cleaning windows, an employee falls from the fourth floor of the building to the   16._____
sidewalk. The custodian finds the man unconscious.
The custodian should

   A. move the man into a more comfortable position near the wall of the building and
   then call a doctor
   B. try to revive the man by depressing his head slightly and applying artificial respira-
   tion
   C. hail a taxi and bring the man to a hospital for treatment
   D. phone for an ambulance and cover the man to keep him warm

17. The duties of a custodian include the knowledge of safety rules to prevent accidents and   17._____
injuries to his employees and himself.
Of the following, the LEAST harmful practice is to

   A. carry a scraper in the pocket with the blade down
   B. measure the cleaning powder with your hands before placing the powder in water
   C. wet the hands before using steel wool
   D. use lye to clean paint brushes

18. The MOST important reason for not wringing out a mop by hand is that   18._____

   A. water cannot be removed effectively in this way
   B. it is not fair to the cleaner
   C. the dirt remains on the mop after the water is removed
   D. pins, nails, or other sharp objects may be picked up and cut the hand, causing an
   infection

19. The method of using a ladder which you would consider LEAST safe is: 19._____

   A. Grasping the side rails of the ladder instead of the rungs when going up
   B. To see that the door is secured wide open when working on a ladder at a door
   C. Leaning weight toward ladder while working on it
   D. Standing on top of the ladder to reach working place

20. When a window pane is broken, the FIRST step the custodian takes is to   20._____

   A. remove broken glass from floors and window sill
   B. determine the cause
   C. remove the putty with a putty knife
   D. prepare a piece of glass to replace the broken pane

21. Your instructions to a cleaner about the proper sweeping of offices should include the fol- 21._____
lowing instruction:

   A. Do not move chairs and wastebaskets from their places when sweeping
   B. Place chairs and baskets on the desks to get them out of the way
   C. Set aside the loose small furniture and chairs in an orderly manner when sweeping
   office floors
   D. Move the desks and chairs to the side of the room close to the wall in order to
   sweep properly

22. To remove dirt accumulations after the completion of the sweeping task, brushes should be   22.____

    A. tapped on the floor in the normal sweeping position
    B. struck on the floor against the side of the block
    C. struck on the floor against the end of the block
    D. turned upside down and the handle tapped on the floor

23. To sweep rough cement floors in a basement, the BEST tool to use is a   23.____

    A. deck brush
    C. corn broom
    B. new 30" floor brush
    D. treated mop

24. When a floor is scrubbed, it is NOT correct to   24.____

    A. use a steady, even rotary motion
    B. rinse the floor with clean hot water
    C. have the mop strokes follow the boards when drying the floor
    D. wet the floor first by pouring several bucketsful of water on it

25. Flushing with a hose is MOST appropriate as a method of cleaning   25.____

    A. terrazzo floors of corridors
    B. untreated wood floors
    C. linoleum floors where not in frequent use
    D. cement floors

KEY (CORRECT ANSWERS)

1.	D		11.	B
2.	D		12.	A
3.	A		13.	A
4.	C		14.	C
5.	B		15.	B
6.	D		16.	D
7.	C		17.	A
8.	A		18.	D
9.	D		19.	D
10.	D		20.	A

21.	C
22.	A
23.	C
24.	D
25.	D

TEST 2

DIRECTIONS: Each question or incomplete statement is followed by several suggested answers or completions. Select the one that BEST answers the question or completes the statement. *PRINT THE LETTER OF THE CORRECT ANSWER IN THE SPACE AT THE RIGHT.*

Questions 1-5.

DIRECTIONS: Column I lists cleaning jobs. Column II lists cleansing agents and devices. Select the proper cleansing agent from Column II for each job in Column I. Place the letter of the cleansing agent selected in the space at the right corresponding to the number of the cleansing job.

COLUMN I   COLUMN II

1. Chewing gum   A. Muriatic acid   1._____
                           B. Broad bladed knife
2. Ink stains   C. Kerosene   2._____
                           D. Oxalic acid
3. Fingermarks on glass   E. Lye   3._____
                           F. Linseed oil
4. Rust stains on porcelain   4._____

5. Hardened dirt on porcelain   5._____

6. When the bristles of a floor brush have worn short, the brush should be   6._____

    A. thrown away and the handles saved
    B. saved and the brush used on rough cement floors
    C. saved and used for high dusting in classrooms
    D. saved and used for the weekly scrubbing of linoleum floors

7. Feather dusters should NOT be used because they   7._____

    A. take more time to use than other dusters
    B. cannot be cleaned
    C. do not take up the dust but merely move it from one place to another
    D. do not stir up the dust and streak the furniture with dust rails

8. Floors that are usually NOT waxed are those made of   8._____

    A. pine wood   B. mastic tile
    C. rubber tile   D. terrazzo

9. For sweeping under radiators and other inaccessible places, the MOST appropriate tool is the   9._____

    A. counter brush   B. dry mop
    C. feather duster   D. 16" floor brush

10. A cleansing agent that should NOT be used in the cleaning of windows is　　10.____

    A. water containing fine pumice
    B. water containing a small amount of ammonia
    C. water containing a little kerosene
    D. a paste cleanser made from water and cleaning powder

11. The BEST way to dust desks is to use a　　11.____

    A. circular motion with soft dry cloth that has been washed
    B. damp cloth, taking care not to disturb papers on the desk
    C. soft cloth, moistened with oil, using a back and forth motion
    D. back and forth motion with a soft dry cloth

12. Trisodium phosphate is a substance BEST used in　　12.____

    A. washing kalsomined walls
    B. polishing of brass
    C. washing mastic tile floors
    D. clearing stoppages

13. Treated linoleum is PROPERLY cleaned by daily　　13.____

    A. dusting with a treated mop
    B. sweeping with a floor brush
    C. mopping with a weak soap solution
    D. mopping after removal of dust with a floor brush

14. Of the following, the MOST proper use for chamois skin is　　14.____

    A. drying of window glass after washing
    B. washing of window glass
    C. polishing of metal fixtures
    D. drying toilet bowls after washing

15. A squeegee is a tool which is used in　　15.____

    A. clearing stoppages in waste lines
    B. the central vacuum cleaning system
    C. cleaning inside boiler surfaces
    D. drying windows after washing

16. Concrete and cement floors are usually painted a battleship gray color. The MOST important reason for painting the floor is　　16.____

    A. to improve the appearance of the floor
    B. the paint prevents the absorption of too much water when the floor is mopped
    C. the paint makes the floor safer and less slippery
    D. the concrete becomes harder and will not settle

17. After a sweeping assignment is completed, floor brushes should be stored　　17.____

    A. in the normal sweeping position, bristles resting on the floor
    B. by hanging the brushes on pegs or nails

C. by piling the brushes on each other carefully in a horizontal position
D. in a dry place after a daily washing

18. Painted walls and ceilings should be brushed down   18._____

   A. daily
   B. weekly
   C. every month, especially during the winter
   D. two or three times a year

19. If an asphalt tile floor becomes excessively dirty, the method of cleaning should include   19._____

   A. the use of kerosene or benzine as a solvent
   B. the use of a solution of modified laundry soda
   C. sanding down the spotted areas with a sanding machine on the wet floor
   D. use of a light oil and treated mop

20. To remove light stains from marble walls, the BEST method is to   20._____

   A. use steel wool and a scouring powder, then rinse with clear warm water
   B. wash the stained area with a dilute acid solution
   C. sand down the spot first, then wash with mild soap solution
   D. wet marble first, then scrub with mild soap solution using a soft fiber brush

21. To rid a toilet room of objectionable odors, the PROPER method is to   21._____

   A. spread some chloride of lime on the floor
   B. place deodorizer cubes in a box hung on the wall
   C. wash the floor with hot water containing a little kerosene
   D. wash the floor with hot water into which some disinfectant has been poured

22. Toilet rooms, to be cleaned properly, should be swept   22._____

   A. daily
   B. and mopped daily
   C. daily and mopped twice a week
   D. daily and mopped thoroughly at the end of the week

23. In waxing a floor, it is usually BEST to   23._____

   A. start the waxing under stationary furniture and then do the aisles
   B. pour the wax on the floor, spreading it under the desks with a wax mop
   C. remove the old wax coat before rewaxing
   D. wet mop the floor after the second coat has dried to obtain a high polish

24. The BEST reason why water should not be used to clean kalsomined walls of a boiler   24._____
    room is that the

   A. walls are usually not smooth and will hold too much water
   B. kalsomine coating does not hold dust
   C. kalsomine coating will dissolve in water and leave streaks
   D. wall brick and kalsomine coating will not dissolve in water and so cannot be
      cleaned

25. In mopping a floor, it is BEST practice to

    A. swing the mop from side to side, using the widest possible stroke across the floor up to the baseboard

    B. swing the mop from side to side, using the widest possible stroke across the floor surface, stopping the stroke from 3 to 5 inches from baseboards

    C. use short, straight strokes, up and back, stopping the strokes about 5 inches from the baseboards

    D. use short straight strokes, up and back, stopping the strokes at the baseboard

25.____

KEY (CORRECT ANSWERS)

1.	B		11.	D
2.	D		12.	C
3.	C		13.	A
4.	A		14.	A
5.	C		15.	D
6.	B		16.	B
7.	C		17.	B
8.	D		18.	D
9.	A		19.	D
10.	A		20.	D

21.	D
22.	B
23.	A
24.	C
25.	B

EXAMINATION SECTION
TEST 1

DIRECTIONS: Each question or incomplete statement is followed by several suggested answers or completions. Select the one that BEST answers the question or completes the statement. *PRINT THE LETTER OF THE CORRECT ANSWER IN THE SPACE AT THE RIGHT.*

1. The BEST of the following substances in which to store used paint brushes is   1.____

   A. gasoline   B. mineral oil
   C. alcohol   D. linseed oil

2. A CORRECT statement with respect to the use of a file is: 2.____

   A. The coarser the tooth of a file, the less metal will be removed on each stroke of the file
   B. Files are generally made to cut in one direction only
   C. When a file is used to pry apart materials, light pressure should be maintained
   D. In filing rounded surfaces, the file should rest on the work at all times

3. An ACCEPTABLE material to use on a door to overcome slight sticking to the door jamb is   3.____

   A. tallow candle   B. graphite
   C. mineral oil   D. #6 oil

4. The PROPER type of wrench to use on plated or polished pipe is a(n) _____ wrench.   4.____

   A. monkey   B. pipe   C. open end   D. strap

5. Of the following, the room which requires the GREATEST amount of illumination per square foot is the   5.____

   A. library   B. gymnasium
   C. auditorium   D. sewing room

6. If one of the electric bulbs in a classroom fails to light up when the switch is snapped, the trouble is MOST likely with the   6.____

   A. switch   B. wiring   C. fuse   D. bulb

7. In general, wood should be fine sanded _____ the grain.   7.____

   A. across   B. diagonal to
   C. with   D. circular to

8. The reason for blowing down the water column of a boiler daily is to   8.____

   A. prevent priming or foaming in the boiler
   B. keep the passages above and below the glass clean
   C. remove lime and other mineral matter from boiler feedwater
   D. reduce the possibility of excess steam pressure from building up

9. A CORRECT step in the procedure of blowing down a low pressure boiler is: 9._____

    A. Close return valves before starting to open the blow-off valve
    B. Start the job while the boiler is in operation
    C. Add fresh water rapidly to reach the maximum level
    D. Close blow-off valve when the water reaches the lowest row of tubes

10. To determine if efficient burning of fuel is occurring, the device which is used is a(n) 10._____

    A. orsat apparatus   B. thermostat
    C. pyrometer   D. bourdon tube

11. The PROPER tool to use to break up clinkers sticking to the grate is a 11._____

    A. shovel   B. slice bar
    C. grate bar   D. rake

12. One of the possible results of closing ash pit doors to regulate draft is 12._____

    A. warping or melting of grates
    B. reduced formation of clinkers
    C. steam will become superheated
    D. live coals will fall into the ash pit

13. Good firing methods require that 13._____

    A. the firebed be thick enough to prevent air from passing through
    B. each side of the grate be kept bare to allow cool air to reach the stack
    C. live coals should not be allowed to burn beneath the grates
    D. the fire be stirred every hour to reduce the amount of unburned gases

14. Of the following, the one that is CORRECT with respect to the burning of hard coal is: 14._____

    A. To prevent clinkers, a hard coal fire should never be poked
    B. The fire bed should not be more than 6 inches thick at any time
    C. Air holes in the bed should be made with a rake or slice bar
    D. Infrequent heavy firing will reduce the possibility of forming holes

15. The MAIN purpose of a Hartford Loop as a return connection for a steam boiler is to 15._____

    A. remove air from the return lines
    B. prevent a boiler from losing its water
    C. allow reduction in boiler header size
    D. reduce friction in return lines

16. If a boiler fails to deliver enough heat, the MOST probable of the following reasons is the 16._____

    A. leaking of the boiler manhole
    B. boiler operating at excessive output
    C. heating surface is covered with soot
    D. unsteady water line as shown by the gauge glass

17. Generally, thermostatic traps of radiators are used to 17._____

    A. prevent the flow of water and air and allow the passage of steam
    B. prevent the passage of steam and allow the passage of water and air

C. stop air from entering the radiator to prevent it from becoming air-bound
D. relieve the radiator of excess steam if pressure rises too high

18. When a heating boiler is in operation, the safety valve should be tested   18._____

A. semi-annually
B. weekly
C. monthly
D. whenever it seems to be stuck

19. In the horizontal rotary cup oil burner, the MAIN purpose of the rotary cup is to   19._____

A. provide air for ignition of the oil
B. pump oil into the burner
C. atomize the oil into small drops
D. turn the flame in a circle to heat the furnace walls evenly

20. The BEST reason for having gaskets on manholes of a boiler is to   20._____

A. prevent leakage from the boiler
B. provide emergency exit for excessive steam pressure
C. provide easy access to the boiler for cleaning
D. prevent corrosion at manholes

21. The MAIN purpose of expansion joints in steam lines is to   21._____

A. provide for changes in length of heated pipe
B. allow for connection of additional radiators
C. provide locations for valves
D. reduce breakage of pipe due to minor movement in the building

22. If too much water is put in a boiler, the result will be   22._____

A. excessive smoke
B. excessive rate of steam output
C. excessive fuel consumption
D. unsteady water line

23. Piping that carries condensate and air from radiators of a heating system is called   23._____

A. dry return if above boiler water line
B. drip line
C. wet return if above boiler water line
D. riser runout

24. Suppose a boiler smokes through the fire door.   24._____
Of the following, the LEAST likely cause is

A. dirty or clogged flues
B. inferior fuel
C. defective chimney draft
D. air leaks into boiler

25. Of the following, the statement concerning accident prevention that is NOT correct is: 25.____

   A. Ladders should be unpainted
   B. Remove finger rings before beginning to mop
   C. Wear loose-fitting clothes when working around boilers or machinery
   D. Set ladder bottom at about 1/5 the ladder length away from the wall against which the ladder rests

———

KEY (CORRECT ANSWERS)

1.	D		11.	B
2.	B		12.	A
3.	A		13.	C
4.	D		14.	A
5.	D		15.	B
6.	D		16.	C
7.	C		17.	B
8.	B		18.	B
9.	B		19.	C
10.	A		20.	A

21.	A
22.	C
23.	A
24.	D
25.	C

———

TEST 2

DIRECTIONS: Each question or incomplete statement is followed by several suggested answers or completions. Select the one that BEST answers the question or completes the statement. *PRINT THE LETTER OF THE CORRECT ANSWER IN THE SPACE AT THE RIGHT.*

1. When the oil burner reset button is pressed, the burner motor does not start.
   The FIRST thing to check is the   1.____

   A. oil supply in oil tanks
   B. possibility of a blown fuse
   C. oil strainers which may be clogged
   D. dirty stack switch

2. When a heating plant is laid up for the summer, one of the steps the fireman should take
   with respect to the boiler is to tap the brace and stay rods with a hammer.
   The MAIN reason for this is to   2.____

   A. clean these parts of accumulated rust and dirt
   B. make certain these parts are in place and not out of line
   C. remove them for storage during summer and early autumn seasons
   D. make certain they are tight and not broken

3. In the event of a bomb threat, the custodian should take the precaution to   3.____

   A. open ash pit and fire doors of boilers
   B. pull the main switch to cut off all power in the building
   C. operate with the least number of water services possible
   D. empty water from boilers immediately after covering fire with ashes

4. The type of fire extinguisher that requires protection against freezing is   4.____

   A. carbon dioxide
   B. carbon tetrachloride (pyrene)
   C. soda acid
   D. calcium chloride

5. A CORRECT procedure in recharging soda acid fire extinguishers is: 5.____

   A. The soda charge should be completed dissolved in 28 gallons of boiling water
   B. The filled acid bottle should be tightly stoppered before it is placed back in the
       extinguisher
   C. The extinguisher must be recharged after use regardless of extent of use
   D. Be sure to fill container with soda solution to the top of container up to threads of
       cap

6. The MOST common cause of slipperiness of a terrazzo floor after being washed is the   6.____

   A. failure to rinse floor clean after cleaning agent is used
   B. destruction of floor seal by cleaning agent
   C. incomplete removal of dirt from the floor
   D. use of oil in the cleaning process

7. When electric lighting fixtures are washed, a precaution to observe is that   7.____

    A. the metal part of the fixture should be washed with a warm mild ammonia solution
    B. the holding screws of glass globes should be loosened about half a turn after cleaning globes
    C. trisodium phosphate should not be used in washing glass globes because it dulls glass
    D. chain links of fixture should be loosened to enable removal of entire fixture

8. Inside burns on recently cut pipe are USUALLY removed by   8.____

    A. filing   B. turning   C. reaming   D. sanding

9. When the average temperature for a day is 48°F, the number of degree days for that day is   9.____

    A. 22   B. 27   C. 12   D. 17

10. Water hammer will MOST likely occur in the   10.____

    A. self-closing valves of a drinking fountain
    B. bends in a pipe line where air can accumulate
    C. globe valve on the supply line to a fixture
    D. angle valve on the steam supply line to a radiator

11. To remove a stoppage in a trap which has not cleared by the use of a force cup, the tool to use is a(n)   11.____

    A. yarning tool   B. auger
    C. expansion bit   D. trowel

12. If the float of a flush tank leaks and fills with water, the MOST probable result will be   12.____

    A. no water in the tank
    B. ball cock remains open
    C. water will flow over the tank rim
    D. flush ball will not seat properly

13. Fresh air inlets are GENERALLY installed in connection with a   13.____

    A. house trap   B. roof vent
    C. sump pump   D. branch soil pipe

14. The PRIMARY function of the water trap in the waste line from a wash bowl is to   14.____

    A. hold excess water from flooding waste line
    B. prevent the flow of sewer gas into the room
    C. catch particles and refuse that may enter the line with the water
    D. provide an easy means for cleaning and repairing the waste line

15. The BEST lubricant for a cylinder lock is   15.____

    A. crude oil   B. machine oil
    C. tallow   D. graphite

16. A window sash holds the   16.____

    A. casing   B. glass   C. jambs   D. sills

17. The BEST procedure to follow to determine the actual cleaning ability of a specific material is to   17.____

    A. test its performance
    B. read the specifications
    C. ask the manufacturer
    D. examine trade literature

Questions 18-21.

DIRECTIONS: Questions 18 through 21 are to be answered on the basis of the following occurrence.

    An accident occured at P.S. 947 on Monday, January 14, resulting in the injury of a fireman-cleaner named John Jones. Jones was found unconscious on the floor of the boiler room. He showed evidence of a head injury. An ambulance was called immediately. Jones was treated by the ambulance attendant, who found no serious injury and treated the head wound. Jones, when asked about the cause of the injury, stated that he had fallen over a coal shovel lying in his path. The head injury apparently resulted from the hard contact of Jones' head with a concrete post. Jones was then taken home and was advised to check with a doctor if he felt groggy or ill. An examination of the boiler room revealed that an electric light located near the scene of the accident was out and that the area was quite dark. There were no witnesses to the accident.

18. Of the following, the information MOST necessary to make the required report on the accident is   18.____

    A. Jones' age
    B. Jones' work habits
    C. the name of the person who found Jones injured
    D. whether Jones was covered by Workmen's Compensation

19. When Jones was found, a safety precaution that should have been taken was   19.____

    A. extinguishing the fire in the furnace
    B. the removal of Jones to a place where the lighting was more satisfactory
    C. avoiding movement of Jones to prevent further injury
    D. raising Jones' head to restore him to consciousness

20. In accordance with Worker's Compensation regulations, Jones has the right to   20.____

    A. compensation if his injuries keep him from work more than one week
    B. use any doctor provided the doctor is approved by the custodian
    C. compensation greater than the amount of his wages if he is seriously injured
    D. compensation only if he proves he did not place the shovel where it was found

21. The MOST important lesson that the custodian should learn from this accident is that   21.____

    A. before an employee starts work, his place of work should be inspected by the custodian
    B. even experienced firemen-cleaners require regular weekly training in the proper performance of their duties

C. employees should be required to turn in old burned out electric bulbs before receiving new ones

D. regular inspections of work spaces are required to reduce accidents to a minimum

22. Information which is of the LEAST value in a report of unlawful entry into a school building is the   22.____

    A. estimated value of missing property
    B. means of entry
    C. time and date of entry
    D. general description of the school building

23. You notice several children marking an entrance door with chalk.
The MOST desirable immediate action to take is to   23.____

    A. stop the children and tell them not to do this again
    B. ask the principal to stop the children from defacing the door
    C. take the names of the children and write to their parents
    D. remove the chalk marks, but say nothing to the children

24. Suppose that the principal advises you that there are peddlers selling their wares at sidewalk locations surrounding the school premises.
The MOST appropriate action to take first is to   24.____

    A. put up signs warning the peddlers that they are violating the law
    B. advise the peddlers that such activity on sidewalks of the school is illegal and to move on
    C. call the police immediately to clear the sidewalks
    D. suggest that the teachers tell their pupils not to patronize these unsupervised peddlers

25. A parent complains that her child refuses to use the school toilet because it is unclean.
The FIRST step you should take upon receipt of the complaint from the school principal is to   25.____

    A. advise the principal that the toilets are kept clean and that the complaint is unwarranted
    B. tell the cleaner in charge of the floor on which the toilet is located to clean the toilet properly
    C. visit the school toilets to check on the statements made in the complaint
    D. ask the parent to see the toilets for herself rather than take the word of her child

KEY (CORRECT ANSWERS)

1.	B		11.	B
2.	D		12.	B
3.	C		13.	A
4.	C		14.	B
5.	C		15.	D
6.	A		16.	B
7.	B		17.	A
8.	C		18.	C
9.	D		19.	C
10.	A		20.	A

21.	D
22.	D
23.	A
24.	B
25.	C

———

EXAMINATION SECTION
TEST 1

DIRECTIONS: Each question or incomplete statement is followed by several suggested answers or completions. Select the one that BEST answers the question or completes the statement. *PRINT THE LETTER OF THE CORRECT ANSWER IN THE SPACE AT THE RIGHT.*

1. Before starting any lawn mowing, the distance between the blade and a flat surface should be measured with a ruler. This distance should be such that the cut of the grass above the ground is _____ inch(es).   1._____

   A.   1   B. $1\frac{1}{2}$ C.   2   D.   3

2. Strainers in a number 6 fuel oil system should be checked once a   2._____

   A.   day   B.   week   C.   month   D.   year

3. The spinning cup on a rotary cup oil burner should be cleaned   3._____

   A.   once a day   B.   once a week
   C.   every 2 weeks   D.   once a month

4. Terrazzo floors should be cleaned daily with a   4._____

   A.   damp mop using clear water
   B.   damp mop using a strong alkaline solution
   C.   damp mop using a mild acid solution
   D.   dust mop treated with vegetable oil

5. New installations of vinyl-asbestos floors should   5._____

   A.   never be machine scrubbed
   B.   be dry buffed weekly
   C.   be swept daily, using an oily compound
   D.   never be swept with treated dust mops

6. Standpipe fire hose shall be inspected   6._____

   A.   monthly   B.   quarterly
   C.   semi-annually   D.   annually

7. All portable fire extinguishers shall be inspected once   7._____

   A.   a year   B.   a month
   C.   a week   D.   every 3 months

8. Soda-acid and foam-type fire extinguishers shall be discharged and recharged AT LEAST once   8._____

   A.   each year   B.   every 2 years
   C.   every 6 months   D.   each month

9. Elevator *safeties* under the car shall be tested once each

    A. day   B. week   C. month   D. quarter

9.____

10. Key-type fire alarms in public school buildings shall be tested

    A. daily   B. weekly   C. monthly   D. quarterly

10.____

11. Combustion efficiency can be determined from an appropriate chart used in conjunction with

    A. steam temperature and steam pressure
    B. flue gas temperature and percentage of CO_2
    C. flue gas temperature and fuel heating value
    D. oil temperature and steam pressure

11.____

12. In the combustion of common fuels, the MAJOR boiler heat loss is due to

    A. incomplete combustion
    B. moisture in the fuel
    C. heat radiation
    D. heat lost in the flue gases

12.____

13. The MOST important reason for blowing down a boiler water column and gauge glass is to

    A. prevent the gauge glass level from rising too high
    B. relieve stresses in the gauge glass
    C. insure a true water level reading
    D. insure a true pressure gauge reading

13.____

14. The secondary voltage of a transformer used for ignition in a fuel oil burner has a range of MOST NEARLY _____ volts to _____ volts.

    A. 120; 240   B. 440; 660
    C. 660; 1,200   D. 5,000; 15,000

14.____

15. Assume that during the month of April there were 3 days with an average outdoor temperature of 30° F, 7 days with 40° F, 10 days with 50° F, 3 days with 60° F, and 7 days with 65°F.
The number of degree days for the month was

    A. 330   B. 445   C. 595   D. 1,150

15.____

16. The pH of boiler feedwater is USUALLY maintained within the range of

    A. 4 to 5   B. 6 to 7   C. 10 to 12   D. 13 to 14

16.____

17. The admission of steam to the coils of a domestic hot water supply tank is regulated by a(n)

    A. pressure regulating valve
    B. immersion type temperature gauge
    C. check valve
    D. thermostatic control valve

17.____

18. The device which senses primary air failure in a rotary cup oil burner is USUALLY called   18.____
a(n)

    A. vaporstate   B. anemometer
    C. venturi   D. pressure gauge

19. The device which starts and stops the flow of oil into an automatic rotary cup oil burner is   19.____
USUALLY called a(n) _____ valve.

    A. magnetic oil   B. oil metering
    C. oil check   D. relief

20. A vacuum breaker, used on a steam heated domestic hot water tank, is USUALLY con-   20.____
nected to the

    A. circulating pump   B. tank wall
    C. aquastat   D. steam coil flange

21. A vacuum pump in a low pressure steam heating system which is equipped with a float   21.____
switch, a vacuum switch, a magnetic starter, and a selector switch, can be operated on

    A. float, vacuum, or automatic
    B. float, vacuum, or continuous
    C. vacuum, automatic, or continuous
    D. float, automatic, or continuous

22. If the temperature of the condensate returning to the vacuum pump in a low pressure   22.____
steam vacuum heating system is above 180° F, the trouble may be caused by

    A. faulty radiator traps
    B. room thermostats being set too high
    C. uninsulated return lines
    D. too many radiators being shut off

23. A feedwater regulator operates to   23.____

    A. shut down the burner when the water is low
    B. maintain the water in the boiler at a predetermined level
    C. drain the water in the boiler
    D. regulate the temperature of the feedwater

24. An automatically fired steam boiler is equipped with an automatic low water cut-off.   24.____
The low water cut-off is USUALLY actuated by

    A. steam pressure   B. fuel pressure
    C. float action   D. water temperature

25. Low pressure steam or an electric heater is USUALLY required for heating _____ fuel   25.____
oil.

    A. #1   B. #2   C. #4   D. #6

KEY (CORRECT ANSWERS)

1.	C		11.	B
2.	A		12.	D
3.	A		13.	C
4.	A		14.	D
5.	B		15.	B
6.	B		16.	C
7.	B		17.	D
8.	A		18.	A
9.	C		19.	A
10.	A		20.	D

21.	D
22.	A
23.	B
24.	C
25.	D

———

TEST 2

DIRECTIONS: Each question or incomplete statement is followed by several suggested answers or completions. Select the one that BEST answers the question or completes the statement. *PRINT THE LETTER OF THE CORRECT ANSWER IN THE SPACE AT THE RIGHT.*

1. A compound gauge is calibrated to read   1._____

    A.   pressure *only*   B.   vacuum *only*
    C.   vacuum and pressure   D.   temperature and humidity

2. In a mechanical pressure-atomizing type oil burner, the oil is automized by using an   2._____
automizing tip and

    A.   steam pressure   B.   pump pressure
    C.   compressed air   D.   a spinning cup

3. A good over-the-fire draft in a natural draft furnace should be *approximately* _____   3._____
inch(es) of water _____.

    A.   5.0; positive pressure   B.   0.05; positive pressure
    C.   0.05; vacuum   D.   5.0; vacuum

4. When it is necessary to add chemicals to a heating boiler, it should be done   4._____

    A.   immediately after boiler blowdown
    B.   after the boiler has been cleaned internally of sludge, scale, and other foreign mat-
       ter
    C.   at periods when condensate flow to the boiler is small
    D.   at a time when there is a heavy flow of condensate to the boiler

5. The modutrol motor on a rotary cup oil burner burning #6 fuel oil automatically operates   5._____
the primary air damper,

    A.   secondary air damper, and oil metering valve
    B.   secondary air damper, and magnetic oil valve
    C.   oil metering valve, and magnetic oil valve
    D.   and magnetic oil valve

6. The manual-reset pressuretrol is classified as a   6._____

    A.   Safety and Operating Control
    B.   Limit and Operating Control
    C.   Limit and Safety Control
    D.   Limit, Operating, and Safety Control

7. Sodium sulphite is added to boiler feedwater to   7._____

    A.   avoid caustic embrittlement
    B.   increase the pH value
    C.   reduce the tendency of foaming in the steam drum
    D.   remove dissolved oxygen

8. Neat cement is a mixture of cement,   8._____

    A. putty, and water   B. and water
    C. lime, and water   D. salt, and water

9. In a concrete mix of 1:2:4, the 2 refers to the amount of   9._____

    A. sand   B. cement   C. stone   D. water

10. The word *natatorium* means MOST NEARLY a(n)   10._____

    A. auditorium   B. playroom
    C. gymnasium   D. indoor swimming pool

11. Plated metal surfaces which are protected by a thin coat of clear lacquer should be   11._____
cleaned with a(n)

    A. abrasive compound   B. liquid polish
    C. mild soap solution   D. lemon oil solution

12. Wet mop filler replacements are ordered by   12._____

    A. length   B. weight
    C. number of strands   D. trade number

13. The BEST way to determine the value of a cleaning material is by   13._____

    A. performance testing
    B. manufacturer's literature
    C. written specifications
    D. interviews with manufacturer's salesman

14. Instructions on a container of cleaning compound state: 14._____
Mix one pound of compound in 5 gallons of water.
Using these instructions, the amount of compound which should be added to 15 quarts
of water is MOST NEARLY _____ ounces.

    A. 3   B. 8   C. 12   D. 48

15. The MOST usual cause of paint blisters is   15._____

    A. too much oil in the paint
    B. moisture under the paint coat
    C. a heavy coat of paint
    D. improper drying of paint

16. The floor that should NOT be machine scrubbed is a(n)   16._____

    A. lobby   B. lunchroom
    C. gymnasium   D. auditorium aisle

17. Pick-up sweeping in a public building is the occasional removal of the more conspicuous   17._____
loose dirt from corridors and lobbies.
This type of sweeping should be done

    A. after scrubbing or waving of floors
    B. with the aid of a sweeping compound

C.   at night after school hours
D.   during regular school hours

18.   According to recommended practice, when a steam boiler is taken out of service for a   18.____
long period of time, the boiler drums should FIRST be

    A.   drained completely while the water is hot (above 212° F)
    B.   drained completely after the water has been cooled down to 180° F
    C.   filled completely without draining
    D.   filled to the level of the top try cock

19.   The prevention and control of vermin and rodents in a building is PRIMARILY a matter of   19.____

    A.   maintaining good housekeeping on a continuous basis
    B.   periodic use of an exterminator's service
    C.   calling in the exterminator when necessary
    D.   cleaning the building thoroughly during school vacation

20.   If it is not possible to plant new shrubs immediately upon delivery in the spring, they   20.____
should be stored in a(n)

    A.   sheltered outdoor area   B.   unsheltered outdoor area
    C.   boiler room   D.   warm place indoors

21.   Peat moss is *generally* used for its   21.____

    A.   food value   B.   nitrogen
    C.   alkalinity   D.   moisture retaining quality

22.   The legal minimum age of employees engaged for cleaning windows in the state is   22.____
_____ years.

    A. 16   B. 17   C. 18   D. 21

23.   The MAIN classification of lumber used for construction purposes is known as _____   23.____
lumber.

    A.   industrial   B.   commercial
    C.   finish   D.   yard

24.   Specifications concerning window cleaners' anchors and safety belts must be in compli-   24.____
ance with the rules and regulations outlined in the

    A.   state labor law and board of standards and appeals
    B.   city building code
    C.   fire department safety manual
    D.   national protection code

25.   Pruning of street trees is the responsibility of the   25.____

    A.   custodian-engineer   B.   board of education
    C.   department of parks   D.   borough president's office

KEY (CORRECT ANSWERS)

1.	C		11.	C
2.	B		12.	B
3.	C		13.	A
4.	D		14.	C
5.	A		15.	B
6.	C		16.	C
7.	D		17.	D
8.	B		18.	B
9.	A		19.	A
10.	D		20.	A

21.	D
22.	C
23.	D
24.	A
25.	C

MECHANICAL APTITUDE
TOOLS AND THEIR USE

EXAMINATION SECTION
TEST 1

DIRECTIONS: Each question or incomplete statement is followed by several suggested answers or completions. Select the one that BEST answers the question or completes the statement. *PRINT THE LETTER OF THE CORRECT ANSWER IN THE SPACE AT THE RIGHT.*

Questions 1-15.

DIRECTIONS: Questions 1 through 15 refer to the tools shown below. The numbers in the answers refer to the numbers beneath the tools.
NOTE: These tools are NOT shown to scale.

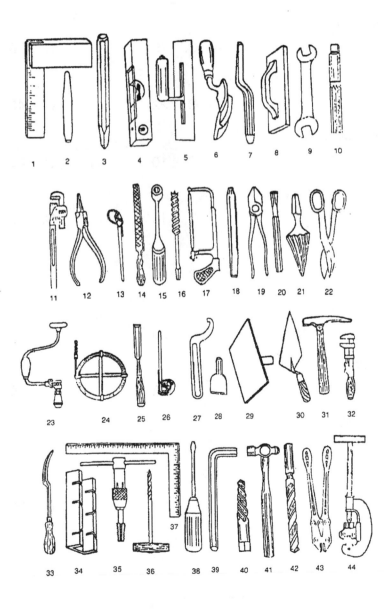

1. A "pipe reamer" is tool number
   A. 2   B. 10   C. 21   D. 24   1.____

2. A "mitre box" is tool number
   A. 1   B. 4   C. 25   D. 34   2.____

3. A "bolt cutter" is tool number
   A. 3   B. 25   C. 40   D. 43   3.____

4. The proper "drill bit" for wood is tool number
   A. 10   B. 16   C. 21   D. 40   4.____

5. A "ball peen" is tool number
   A. 20   B. 31   C. 33   D. 41   5.____

6. A "hawk" is tool number
   A. 5   B. 28   C. 29   D. 30   6.____

7. "Snips" is tool number
   A. 12   B. 19   C. 22   D. 43   7.____

8. A "bull point" is tool number
   A. 3   B. 7   C. 10   D. 20   8.____

9. An "open-end wrench" is tool number
   A. 9   B. 11   C. 15   D. 27   9.____

10. A "drift pin" is tool number
    A. 2   B. 3   C. 10   D. 40   10.____

11. A "pipe cutter" is tool number
    A. 17   B. 18   C. 28   D. 44   11.____

12. A "trowel" is tool number
    A. 6   B. 8   C. 28   D. 30   12.____

13. A "square" is tool number
    A. 4   B. 29   C. 34   D. 37   13.____

14. A "float" is tool number
    A. 8   B. 28   C. 29   D. 30   14.____

15. A "snake" is tool number
    A. 13   B. 24   C. 26   D. 36   15.____

KEY (CORRECT ANSWERS)

1.	C	6.	C
2.	D	7.	C
3.	D	8.	A
4.	B	9.	A
5.	D	10.	A

11.	D
12.	D
13.	D
14.	A
15.	B

———

TEST 2

DIRECTIONS: Each question or incomplete statement is followed by several suggested answers or completions. Select the one that BEST answers the question or completes the statement. *PRINT THE LETTER OF THE CORRECT ANSWER IN THE SPACE AT THE RIGHT.*

1. The tool shown at the right is a
   A. countersink
   B. counterbore
   C. star drill
   D. burring reamer

   1._____

2. The saw shown at the right would be used to cut
   A. curved designs in thin wood
   B. strap iron
   C. asphalt tiles to fit against walls
   D. soft lead pipe

   2._____

3. The tool shown at the right is a
   A. float
   B. finishing trowel
   C. hawk
   D. roofing seamer

   3._____

4. The hammer shown to the right would be used by a
   A. carpenter
   B. bricklayer
   C. tinsmith
   D. plumber

   4._____

5. When drilling into a steel plate, the *most likely* cause for the breaking of a drill bit is

   A. too low a drill speed   B. excessive cutting oil lubricant
   C. too much drill pressure   D. using a bit with a dull point

   5._____

6. Of the following, the *most important* advantage of a ratchet wrench over an open-end wrench is that the ratchet wrench

   A. can be used in a more limited space
   B. measures the torque applied
   C. will not strip the threads of a bolt
   D. is available for all sizes of hex bolts

   6._____

7. The tool that holds the die when threading pipe is *generally* called a

   A. vise   B. stock   C. yoke   D. coupling

   7._____

8. A fitting used to join a small pipe at right angles to the middle of a large pipe is called a

   A. union   B. coupling   C. cap   D. reducing tee

   8._____

9. Gaskets are *commonly* used between the flanges of large pipe joints to   9.____

    A. make a leakproof connection   B. provide for expansion
    C. provide space for assembly   D. adjust for poor alignment

10. The pipe fitting that should be used to connect a 1" pipe to a 1 1/2" valve is called a   10.____

    A. reducing coupling   B. nipple
    C. bushing   D. union

11. The part of a drill press which is used to hold the drill bit is called a   11.____

    A. chuck   B. collar   C. bit   D. vise

12. When grinding a flat chisel, it is *good* practice to keep the chisel moving across the face   12.____
of the grinding wheel in order to prevent

    A. grooving of the wheel   B. burning of the chisel tip
    C. the wheel from vibrating   D. the wheel from cracking

13. In order to determine if a surface is *truly* horizontal, it should be checked with a   13.____

    A. carpenter's square   B. plumb bob
    C. steel rule   D. spirit level

14. A gauge of a nail indicates the   14.____

    A. length of the shank   B. diameter of the head
    C. thickness of the head   D. diameter of the shank

15. A tool that can be used *both* for scribing regular arcs and also for transferring dimensions   15.____
is the

    A. trammel   B. protractor
    C. scriber   D. combination square

16. The devices for clamping sheet metal in place on a squaring shear are the   16.____

    A. clamps   B. hold-downs   C. guides   D. square

17. When a hacksaw is used to cut sheet metal, the BEST blade to use is one with _____   17.____
teeth per inch.

    A. 14   B. 18   C. 24   D. 32

18. A tool which may be attached to a drill press and used to cut circles of 2 1/2" diameter or   18.____
larger in sheet metal is the

    A. twist drill   B. circular saw   C. reamer   D. hole saw

19. A versatile hand tool that can be used for a variety of sheet metalwork jobs such as buck-   19.____
ing up rivet heads, straightening kinks in formed metal, forming seams, etc., is the

    A. hand dolly   B. universal iron worker
    C. cupping tool   D. set hammer

20. To make certain two points separated by a vertical distance of 8 feet are in perfect vertical alignment, it would be BEST to use a(n)   20.____

    A. surface gage   B. height gage
    C. protractor   D. plumb bob

21. A claw hammer is PROPERLY used for   21.____

    A. driving a cold chisel   B. driving brads
    C. setting rivets   D. flattening a 1/2" metal bar

22. It would NOT be good practice to tighten a 1" hexagon nut with a(n) _____ wrench.   22.____

    A. monkey   B. 1" fixed open-end
    C. adjustable open-end   D. stillson

23. Lock washers are used PRINCIPALLY with _____ screws.   23.____

    A. machine   B. wood   C. self-tapping   D. lag

24. Toggle bolts are MOST appropriate for use to fasten conduit clamps to a   24.____

    A. steel column   B. concrete wall
    C. hollow tile wall   D. brick wall

25. If a 10-24 by 3/4" machine screw is not available, the screw which could be *most easily* modified to use in an emergency is a   25.____

    A. 10-24 by 1/2"   B. 12-24 by 3/4"
    C. 10-24 by 1 1/2"   D. 8-24 by 3/4"

26. Of the following tools, the *one* that should be used to cut thin-wall metal tubing is the   26.____

    A. reamer   B. plier   C. hacksaw   D. broach

27. A wrench than can be used to tighten a nut to a specified tightness is a _____ wrench.   27.____

    A. bonney   B. spud   C. torque   D. adjustable

28. The *one* of the following that will *most likely* show a "mushroomed" head is a   28.____

    A. cold chisel   B. file cleaner
    C. screwdriver blade   D. ratchet

29. A tool that is used to bend pipe is the   29.____

    A. lintel   B. hickey   C. collet   D. brace

30. *Before* drilling a hole in a steel plate, an indentation should be made with a   30.____

    A. center punch   B. nail   C. drill bit   D. pin punch

KEYS (CORRECT ANSWERS)

1.	D	16.	B
2.	A	17.	D
3.	A	18.	D
4.	B	19.	A
5.	C	20.	D
6.	A	21.	B
7.	B	22.	D
8.	D	23.	A
9.	A	24.	C
10.	C	25.	C
11.	A	26.	C
12.	A	27.	C
13.	D	28.	A
14.	D	29.	B
15.	A	30.	A

———

BASIC CLEANING PROCEDURES

TABLE OF CONTENTS

		Page
I.	TRASH REMOVAL	1
II.	CLEANING URNS AND ASHTRAYS	5
III.	DUSTING	7
IV.	FLOOR DUSTING	14
V.	VACUUMING (WET AND DRY)	16
VI.	MOPPING (WET, DAMP, SPOT)	18

BASIC CLEANING PROCEDURES

I. TRASH REMOVAL

PURPOSE: To remove waste from patient and tenant areas in order to provide the highest standard of sanitation; protection against fire, pests, odor, bacteria, and other health hazards; and for esthetic reasons.

EQUIPMENT:

Utility cart
Trash cart
Bucket
Germicidal detergent
Plastic liners (small and large)
Cloths
Gloves
Container for cigarette butts

SAFETY PRECAUTIONS:

1. Must wear gloves.

2. Never handle trash with bare hands.

3. Always empty cigarette butts into separate container that has water or sand in it.

4. If liners are not used, do not transfer trash from one container to another transfer trash into a liner. (Shown in Illustration.)

5. Trash must be separated into two categories: General and Special.
   General

PROCEDURE

General

1. Assemble necessary equipment, prepare ger-micidal solution, and take to assigned area.

2. Put on gloves.

3. Pick up large trash on floor, place in trash container.

4. Close plastic liner and secure with tie.

5. Remove liner and place in trash bag on utility cart or place into trash cart, or other trash collection vehicle.

PROCEDURE

6. Emerge (dip) cloth into germicidal solution. Wring out thoroughly.

7. Wipe outside and inside of trash container. Dry with second cloth.

8. Replace liner. Liner should extend over top of trash container and fold outward over the upper rim. If plastic liners are not being used, use the Replacement Method-a clean container is exchanged for the dirty one.

9. Proceed with this procedure until all trash is collected or containers are full.

10. Place in utility room or an appropriate storage area until time for disposal.

11. Remove trash from the storage area at the end of the day or at some specified time (by cart or dolly) to dumpsters.

12. If large G.I. cans are used in the specified trash storage area, maintain as listed above.

13. At least once a month, take all trash cans to a specified area and thoroughly wash or steam clean.

14. If using the Replacement Method, dirty trash containers must be washed or steam cleaned daily. Must be stored in inverted or upside-down position to air dry.

15. Clean all equipment and return to designated storage area. Restock utility cart.

PROCEDURE

Special
Waste Handling
Syringes-Hypodermic Needles-
Razor Blades

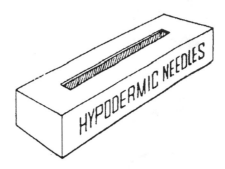

1. Collect from specified areas (full dispos-
    able containers designed for this waste).

2. Place in 20-gallon galvanized container
    in locked designated area.

3. Call Garage for pick up and disposal
    when galvanized container is full (10).

Glass and Aerosol Cans

1. Collect from designated areas in marked
    metal containers.

2. Place in 20-gallon galvanized containers
    in locked designated area daily.

3. Call Garage for pick up and disposal
    when container is full.

Pathological Specimen
(Tissue-flesh)

1. This type of waste is handled by a spe-
    cial technologist in the Hospital's Patho-
    logical Division.

2. Must be stored in refrigerator until
    incinerated.

3. Must be incinerated in special incinerator
    designed for this purpose.

PROCEDURE

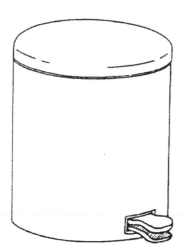

Contaminated

The same procedure is used as for general collection with the following exceptions:

1. Must have covered step-on containers.

2. A second person is required to hold clean liner (top folded over hands for protection).

3. The tied soiled plastic liner is removed from the waste container and placed in a clean plastic liner and then deposited into the regular trash.

4. If in areas that are restricted, must wear protective garments.

II. CLEANING URNS AND ASHTRAYS

PURPOSE: To prevent fire hazards, to control bacteria, and for appearance.

EQUIPMENT:

    Utility cart
    Sifter or slit spoon
    Bucket for sand
    Cloths or Sponges
    Container for cigarette butts
    Gloves
    Buckets (two)
    Counter brush and dustpans
    Germicidal detergent

SAFETY PRECAUTIONS:

1. Wear gloves.
2. Do not place plastic liners on inside of urns.
3. Sweep up all spilled sand immediately.
4. Make sure cigarette butts are placed in special container with water or sand in the bottom.

PROCEDURE

1. Assemble equipment. Prepare solution. Take to designated area.

2. Put on gloves.

3. Empty ashtrays. Dip ashtrays into solution. Wash. Rinse in clear water. Dry. Return to proper area.

4. Continue cleaning other cigarette receptacles. Receptacles can be smoke stands, and/or wall and floor urns with or without sand.

    a. Smoke stands and wall urns:

    (1) Empty cigarette butts into special container (by lifting out inside bucket or unscrewing base from top).

    (2) Wash, rinse, and dry the base, top, bucket and wall attachment.

SAND FOR ASHES

PROCEDURE

b. Floor urns with sand:

(1) Take out large pieces of trash.

(2) Lift screen to remove cigarette butts and any other waste. Use sifter and spoon for this procedure if screens are not in use.

5. Replace sand if necessary. Sweep up any spilled sand.

6. Dip cloth into germicide solution. Wring out. Wipe off rim and outside of urns. Rinse and dry.

7. Continue this procedure until all urns are completed.

8. Clean all equipment and return to designated storage.

9. At least once a month collect cigarette receptacles. Take to utility room. Remove sand where applicable. Submerge in germicidal solution. Wash thoroughly. Rinse and dry. Replace sand and return to designated areas.

III. DUSTING

PURPOSE: To remove accumulated soil, to control bacteria, for protection, and for appearance.

EQUIPMENT:

    Utility cart
    Treated cloths
    Germicidal detergent
    Gloves
    Furniture polish
    Sweeping tool or Broom
    Extension handle
    Clean cloths
    Buckets (two)
    Vacuum cleaner (Wet and Dry or Back
    Pack) Broom bags

SAFETY PRECAUTIONS:

1. A fold dust cloth is more efficient than a bunched cloth. When folded properly, a cloth may have as many as 32 clean sides.

2. Use treated cloths or damp cloths when dusting. (Never use a feather duster.)

3. Oily cloths are fire hazards: they must be stored in a covered container.

4. Never shake cloth.

5. Never use circular motion. Dust with the grain.

6. Never use excessive water on wood furniture.

7. Do not take dust cloth from one patient unit to the next.

PROCEDURE

General-Dry

1. Assemble equipment. Prepare solution. Take to assigned area.

2. Put on gloves.

3. Fold treated cloth or damp germicidal cloth. (If using the damp germicidal cloth, use a second cloth for polishing.)

PROCEDURE

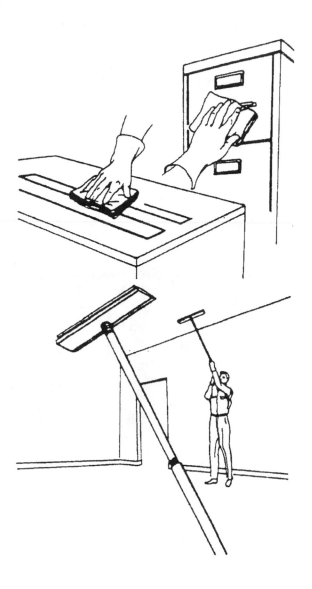

4. Look at area. Begin dusting at a point to avoid backtracking. Use both hands whenever possible. Begin with high furniture and work down to low furniture (for example, dust file cabinets before dusting desk tops).

5. Refold cloth when sides become dust filled or refresh by returning to germicidal solution.

6. Continue dusting until area is completed.

7. Inspect work.

8. Clean equipment and return to designated storage area. Cleaning cloths are placed in liner for laundering; woven treated paper dust cloths are discarded.

Wall and Ceiling Dusting

1. Assemble equipment. Take to assigned area.

2. Move furniture that will interfere with operation to one side of the room. Remove all pictures and other wall mountings and place in a safe area.

3. Put on gloves.

4. Dust ceiling. Start at back of room. Use vacuum or Floor tool or covered broom with extension handle. Place dusting tool against ceiling surface and walk forward to the other end.

5. Turn and overlap stroke. Continue this proc-dure until completed.

6. Dust ceiling both cross-wise and length-wise.

PROCEDURE

7. When ceiling is completed, dust walls from top to bottom. Use full-length vertical overlapping strokes. Include vents, ledges and exposed pipes.

8. When one side of area is completed, replace furniture.

9. Move furniture from other side and continue the dusting procedure until entire area is completed.

10. Replace furniture, pictures and other wall mountings.

11. Inspect work.

12. Clean equipment. Return to designated storage areas. Broom bags are placed in plastic liner/bag for laundering; woven treated paper dust cloths are discarded.

General Comments for Dusting Different Types of Furniture

1. Wooden Furniture:
    a. Dust entire surface.

    b. Apply polish-pour small amount on damp cloth-rub with grain.

    c. Finish polishing by rubbing with dry cloth.

    d. Surface may be washed with natural detergent.

CAUTION: Excessive amount of water should be avoided.

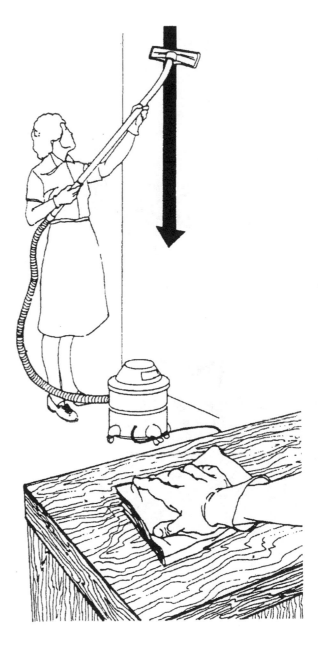

PROCEDURE

2. Metal Furniture:

   a. Dust entire surface.

   b. Surface may be washed and polished.

   c. Apply polish-pour small amount on damp cloth-rub in.

   d. Polish/rub thoroughly with a second cloth.

3. Plastic, Vinyl or Fiber Glass:

   a. Dust entire surface.

   b. Wash with germicidal cleaning solution.

   c. Rinse.

   d. Rub surface dry.

4. Leather:

   a. Damp dust.

   b. Clean with leather polish or saddle soap.

5. Upholstered Pieces:

   a. Vacuum entire surface thoroughly. Use push-pull strokes.

   b. Lift cushion-vacuum both sides, cushion support, and bottom of chair. Do not overlook corners and crevices.

   c. Check carefully for stains and report to supervisor.

PROCEDURE

Naugahyde:

    a. Elastic:

(1) Ordinary Dirt-Ordinary dirt can be removed by washing with warm water and a mild soap. Apply soapy water to a large area and allow to soak for a few minutes. This will loosen the dirt. Brisk rubbing with a cloth should then remove most dirt. This procedure may be repeated several times if necessary.

In the case of stubborn or imbedded dirt in the grain of the Naugahyde, a finger-nail brush or other soft bristle brush may be used after the mild soap application has been made.

If the dirt is extremely difficult to remove, wall washing preparations may be used. Abrasive cleaners may also be used. Abrasive cleaners should be used more cautiously and care exercised to prevent contact with the wood or metal parts of furniture or with any soft fabric which may be a part of the furniture.

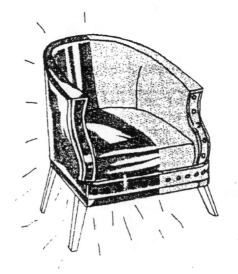

(2) Chewing gum-Chewing gum may be removed by careful scraping and by applying kerosene, gasoline or naphtha. If none of these are available, most hair oils or Three-In-One oil will soften the chewing gum so that it may be removed.

(3) Tars, Asphalts. Creosote-Each of these items will stain Naugahyde if allowed to remain in contact. They should be wiped off as quickly as possible and the area carefully cleaned with a cloth dampened with kerosene, range oil, gasoline or naphtha.

(4) Paint-Paint should be removed immediately if possible. Do not use paint remover or liquid type brush cleaners. An unprinted cloth dampened with kerosene, painters naphtha or turpentine may be used. Care must be exercised to keep these fluids from contact with

PROCEDURE

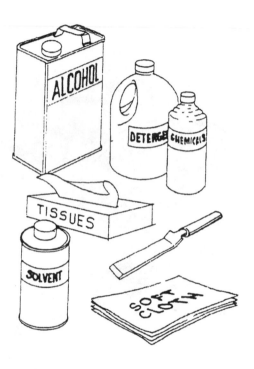

soft fabrics or with the wooden areas of the furniture.

(5) Sulphide Staining-Atmosphere permeated with coal gas or direct contact with hard-boiled eggs, "Cold Wave" solutions and other sulphide compounds can stain Naugahyde. These stains may be removed by placing a clean, unprinted piece of cloth over the spotted area and pouring a liberal amount of 6% hydrogen peroxide onto the cloth and allowing the saturated cloth to remain on the spotted area for at least thirty minutes to one hour. If spot is stubborn, allow the hydrogen peroxide saturated cloth to remain on the spotted area overnight. Caution must be used to see that the hydrogen peroxide solution does not come in contact with stained or lacquered wood and should not be allowed to seep into the seams as it will weaken the cotton thread.

(6) Nail Polish and Nail Polish Remover-These substances will cause permanent harm to Naugahyde on prolonged contact. Fast and careful wiping or blotting immediately after contact will minimize the staining. Spreading of the liquid while removing should be avoided.

(7) Shoe Polish-Most shoe polishes contain dyes which will penetrate the Naugahyde and stain it permanently. They should be wiped off as quickly as possible using kerosene, gasoline, naphtha or lighter fluid. If staining occurs, the same procedure outlined above for sulphide staining using hydrogen peroxide should be tried.

(8) Shoe Heel Marks-Shoe heel marks can be removed by the same procedure as is recommended for paint.

(9) Ball Point Ink-Ball point ink may sometimes be removed if rubbed immediately with a damp cloth using water or

PROCEDURE

rubbing alcohol. If this is not successful, the procedure outlined for sulphide staining may be tried.

(10) Generally stains are found which do not respond to any of the other treatments, it is sometimes helpful to place the furniture in direct sunlight for two or three days. Mustard, ball point ink, certain shoe polishes and dyes will sometimes bleach out in direct sunlight and leave the Naugahyde undamaged.

(11) Waxing or Refinishing-Waxing improves the soil resistance and cleanability of Naugahyde. and any solid wax may be used.

b. Breathable:

U.S. Naugaweave should be treated as a soft fabric and not as a fully vinyl coated fabric. U.S. Naugaweave can be cleaned with foam type cleansers generally used for soft fabrics.

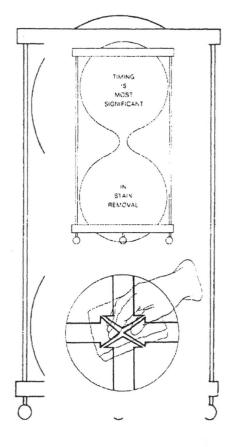

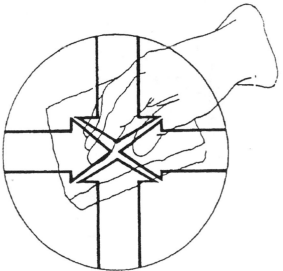

IV. FLOOR DUSTING
(Sweeping/Dusting with covered broom or floor tool with chemically treated disposable floor cloth)

PURPOSE: To remove surface dirt, and make washing easier.

EQUIPMENT:
- Utility cart
- Dustpan
- Treated cloths, or
- Broom bags
- Counter brush
- Sweeping tool, or
- Vacuum cleaner

SAFETY PRECAUTIONS:
1. Never leave piles of dirt and trash in any area.
2. Lift sweeping tool at the end of each stroke. *Do not tap.*
3. Never put waste or sweepings in a patient's waste basket.
4. Keep all equipment out of traffic areas.
5. Use of disposable cloths should be limited to two surfaces (i.e. use two treated cloths per ward, and two Administrative units can be cleaned with one cloth).

PROCEDURE

1. Assemble equipment. Take to assigned area.

2. Move furniture, if necessary.

3. Start dusting/sweeping at far end of room or area and work toward door.

4. Place floor tool on direct line with right toe. Hold handle loosely. Stand erect with feet about eight inches apart. Start dusting/sweeping floor-walking forward. Use a push stroke, lift tool at end of each stroke. Do not tap. Overlap each stroke.

PROCEDURE

5. Continue this procedure until area is completed. Clean under all stationary equipment and furniture.

6. Take up accumulated dirt. Use dustpan and counter brush. Place in plastic liner/ trash bag on utility cart.

7. The dusting/sweeping procedure can be performed with the wet and dry vacuum cleaner. *Dusting Isolation units must be performed with vacuum.*

8. Inspect work. Floor should not have any dust streaks. Replace furniture.

9. Clean equipment. Return to designated storage area. Discard disposable treated cloths. If broom bags are used, place in plastic liner/bag for laundering.

V. VACUUMING
(Wet and Dry)

PURPOSE: To remove dust and dirt and water, to control the spread of bacteria, to aid in reaching difficult-to-reach areas, and for appearance. This operation may be performed on floors, walls, ceiling, rugs, and carpets.

EQUIPMENT:
Upright or tank vacuum cleaner

Wet and dry vacuum cleaner

Back-pack vacuum cleaner

Attachments: Crevice tool, Shelf brush, Pipe brush, Upholstery brush, Walls and Ceiling brush, Dusting brush, and Floor-dry and wet tools.

SAFETY PRECAUTIONS:

1. Empty vacuum when bag is half full.

2. If disposable bag is not in use, empty soil into plastic liner/bag.

3. Never position equipment so that it becomes a tripping hazard.

PROCEDURE

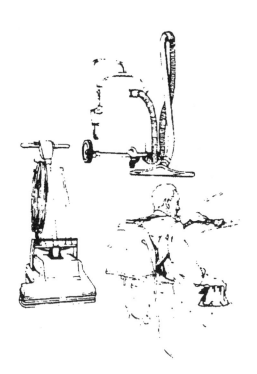

Dry

1. Assemble proper equipment and attachments for the area to be vacuumed:

    a. Upright vacuum for carpet.

    b. Tank cleaner to use on floors, grooves and high cleaning.

    c. Back-pack for stairs, hard to reach areas, walls and ceiling, and drapery.

2. Remove all furniture and other items interfering with the operation.

3. Start in farthest corner of room, area or top of item. Vacuum the surface in a back-and-forth motion.

PROCEDURE

4. Empty bag when half full. Continue this procedure until area or item is completed. Change attachments as required.

5. Replace furniture or items.

6. Take equipment to utility room. Empty and clean. Return to designated storage area.

Wet

This procedure is used to remove water. It is considered very effective in the daily performance of different tasks in order to control the spread of infectious organisms. Wet vacuuming is often used in emergencies-flooding, pipe breaks and overflows. See vacuum cleaner guide under Care of Equipment for operation of the wet vacuum.

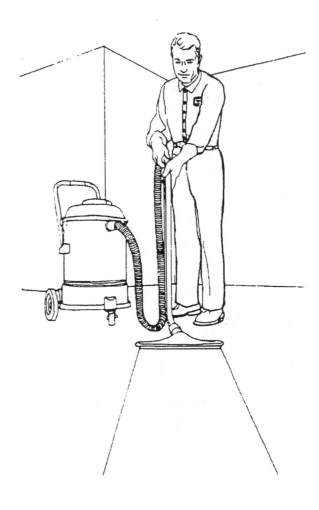

VI . Mopping
(Wet, Damp, Spot)

PURPOSE: To insure maximum cleanliness, to improve the sanitation of the environment, to aid in control of bacteria, and for the appearance of the area.

MATERIALS:

Utility cart
Buckets (two)
Dolly
Wringers (two)
Mopheads and Handles (two)
Nylon abrasive pad
Caution signs
Gloves
Broom-Broom bags
Sweeping tool-treated cloths
Wet and dry vacuum cleaner
Putty knife
Dustpan
Counter brush
Germicidal detergent

SAFETY PRECAUTIONS:

1. Sweep or vacuum before mopping.

2. Post area with "Wet Floor" signs.

3. Mop one-half of corridor at a time.

4. Keep equipment close to walls and away from doors and corners.

5. Excessive water should not be allowed to remain on the floor for any length of time because it will cause damage to nearly all types of flooring material.

6. Begin the operation with clean equipment, mopheads, and clean solution.

7. Change cleaning solution and rinse water frequently (every three to four rooms, depending on size and soilage factors).

8. Solution containers should be conveniently positioned so as not to cause tripping or walking over cleaned areas.

PROCEDURE

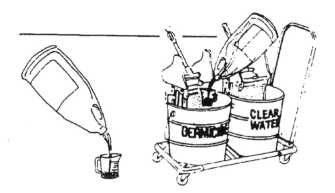

Wet Mopping

1. Assemble equipment. Fill one container two-thirds full with water. Add recommended amount of germicidal detergent. Fill second container two-thirds full with clear water.

19

PROCEDURE

2. Proceed to designated work area. Post "Wet Floor" signs. Move furniture to simplify operation. Vacuum or dust area with covered broom or tool with treated cloth. Remove gum with putty knife. (Use dustpan and counter brush to remove debris and trash.)

3. Dip one mop into cleaning solution and press out excess water to prevent dripping.

4. First, apply solution on and along baseboard or coving. Use the heel of mop-tiead to clean baseboard and corners. (The putty knife can be used to clean out heavily soiled corners or strands of the mophead wrapped around gloved fingertips is another tool for cleaning the corners. A baseboard scrubber or an improvised abrasive pad on a mop handle can be used to remove built-up soil on baseboards.)

5. Return mop to germicidal solution. Churn thoroughly, wring out and pick up solution off baseboards. Apply rinse water with second mop and dry.

6. Continue with the mopping operation. Take solution mop (with excess water pressed out) and make an eight-inch border around floor area approximately nine feet wide and twelve feet long.

7. Begin at top of area. Place mop flat on floor, feet well apart, place right hand-palm up, almost two inches from end of handle, and left hand-palm down, about fourteen inches on handle. Begin swinging mop from left to right or right to left using a continuous open figure-eight motion. At the end of approximately six to nine strokes (width of strokes depend on height and weight of worker), turn mop over or renew direction by lapping mop (lift mophead and loop it over the strands). Continue this procedure until area is completed. (A nylon pad attached to one side of mophead can be used to remove black marks while performing the daily mopping procedure.

PROCEDURE

8. Return mop to germicidal solution. Churn thoroughly. Wring out and pick up solution. Use same procedure as for applying solution.

9. Dip the second mop into the rinse water, press out excess water and apply rinse water to area. Use same procedure for rinsing as for applying cleaning solution.

10. Dip the second mop again into rinse water, wring out thoroughly and dry floor using side-to-side stroke.

11. Continue the four steps of mopping, picking up, rinsing, and drying until the area has been covered. Change cleaning solution and rinse water frequently.

12. Inspect work: A properly mopped floor should have a clean surface. There should be no water spots. The corners should be clean and baseboards should not be splashed.

13. Wash and dry equipment and return to designated storage area.

14. Mopheads are removed and placed in a plastic bag, and then placed in a regular laundry bag and stored in the designated area to be picked up and laundered.

PROCEDURE

Damp Mopping

Damp mopping is a type of mopping used to remove surface dust. This procedure may be used in place of dry dust mopping. Each time mop is dipped into solution or rinse water, it is wrung out thoroughly. The same motions are carried out in this procedure as are for the wet mopping.

Spot Mopping

Spot mopping is a type of mopping used only when a small area is soiled by spillage (water, coke, coffee, urine and other liquids). Spillage must be wiped up immediately in order to prevent slipping and falling hazards. First, absorb liquid with paper towels or blotters, then mop area.

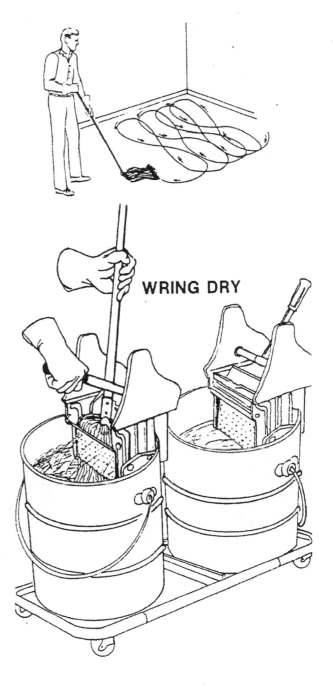

WRING DRY

SPECIAL CLEANING PROCEDURES

TABLE OF CONTENTS

Page

I.   Drinking Fountain   1

II.   Moving Furniture and Equipment   2

III.   Cleaning Drapery, Venetian Blinds and Window Shades   5

IV.   Glass and Window Cleaning   9

V.   Cleaning Light Fixtures (Fluorescent and Globes)   12

VI.   Wall Washing (Manual and Machine)   15

VII.   Cleaning Elevators   19

VIII.   Entrance and Lobby Cleaning   21

IX.   Stairs and Stairwells, Porches and Back Entrances
     (Wet and Dry)   24

SPECIAL CLEANING PROCEDURES

I. DRINKING FOUNTAIN

PURPOSE: To control the spread of bacteria and for appearance.

EQUIPMENT:
Germicidal detergent

Paper towels
Buckets (two)
Abrasive cleanser
Bottle brush
Cloths
Gloves

PROCEDURE

1. Assemble equipment. Prepare solution. Take to designated area. Put on gloves.

2. Check water flow.

3. Pour some germicidal solution into bubbler/ mouthpiece and inside surfaces.

4. Scrub bubbler inside and outside with bottle brush.

5. Wash inside surface with paper towel. (Use small amount of abrasive cleanser, if applicable.)

6. Rinse with water from bubbler/mouthpiece. Dry with paper towel.

7. Wash outside surfaces including foot pedal.

8. Rinse and dry.

9. Discard soiled paper towels.

10. Continue with next assignment or clean equipment and return to designated storage area.

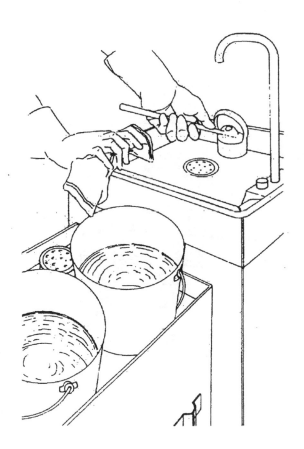

II. MOVING FURNITURE AND EQUIPMENT

PURPOSE: To relocate.

However, for proper maintenance purposes, the Housekeeping Section is involved daily with some form of the moving operation which involves moving of furniture and equipment (desks, file cabinets, beds and other items).

EQUIPMENT: Lifting Aids:
    Desk lifter
    File cabinet lifter
    Dolly
    Cart or Table on wheels
    Blanket
    Straps

SAFETY PRECAUTIONS:

1. Secure all locks and safety adjustments on equipment before using.

2. Remove handles or straps that interfere with the operation.

3. Block or lock all wheels on movable carts or tables.

4. To transport objects on movable table or cart, walk down center of hall; stop at corners, watch swinging doors.

5. Do not block vision.

6. Only properly trained individuals should use specialized moving equip- ment.

General

PROCEDURE

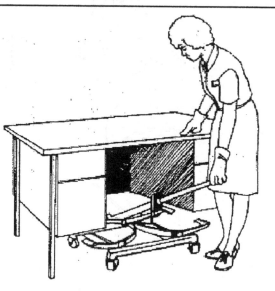

1. Assemble necessary equipment and take to assigned area.

2. Prepare the area (move anything inter-fering with the move).

3. Place lifting aid as close as possible to the piece of furniture or object being relocated.

4. Place object on lifting aid and transport to new location.

5. Return lifting aids and accessories to designated storage area.

PROCEDURE

1. Place under desk and center evenly on arms.

2. Lock. Press down on handle to lift and lock.

3. Remove handle.

4. Move desk to new location.

5. Remove desk lifter. (Insert handle, press down to release safety lock, lower desk into position, and withdraw desk lifter.) Return to designated storage area.

File Cabinet Lifter

1. Adjust bar and lifter head to height of cabinet.

2. Insert lifting blade under file cabinet.

3. Rest lifter head qn top of cabinet.

4. Press lifter tightly against cabinet and adjust arm on the lifter head to fit cabinet top by turning the two wheels.

5. Pull down level on adjustment bar to secure arm and the lifter head.

6. Pivot forward until locked into resting position.

7. Place one hand on bar and the other on handle; press down until cabinet clears the floor.

PROCEDURE

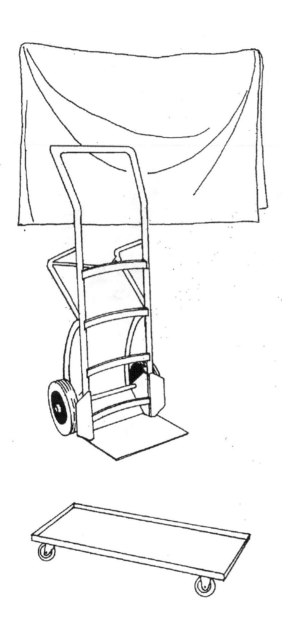

8. Roll into new position.

9. Remove lifter (raise lever arm in upright position, release lifter head by raising the side of the head assembly and remove lifter). Return to designated storage area.

10. To relocate taller cabinets, completely remove the lifter head bar asembly.

- -

**Other Methods
Blankets, Dollies, Carts or
Tables on wheels**

Quite frequently, you may lack the above-mentioned sophisticated equipment. Therefore, you should also know that just by placing a blanket under a desk, table, bookend, file cabinet and other heavy objects, that the item may be pushed or pulled into a new location. If moving over carpeted areas, first place a piece of cardboard down. If using dollies or tables or carts, make sure that furniture or dollies are covered in order to protect from damage.

III. CLEANING DRAPERY, VENETIAN BLINDS AND WINDOW SHADES

PURPOSE: To control bacteria and for appearance.

EQUIPMENT:

    Vacuum cleaner/attachments
    Cart
    Germicidal detergent
    Gloves
    Six-foot step ladder
    Cloths
    Buckets (two)
    Venetian blind brush

SAFETY PRECAUTIONS:

1. Vacuuming should not be done too often, because it weakens the fiber of the fabric.

2. Always cover hands when cleaning Venetian blinds, because of the sharp edges.

PROCEDURE

Drapery

1. Assemble equipment. Take to designated area. Set up ladder and lock.

2. Connect vacuum to nearest convenient outlet.

3. Remove tie-backs and close the draperies.

4. Vacuum. Start at top of cornice or at top of drapery and work down. Use up-and-down motions—overlap.

5. Pull pleats apart to reach all surfaces.

6. Continue this procedure until front of drapery is completed.

7. Pull out drapery and dust the back side. Pull pleats apart to reach all surfaces.

PROCEDURE

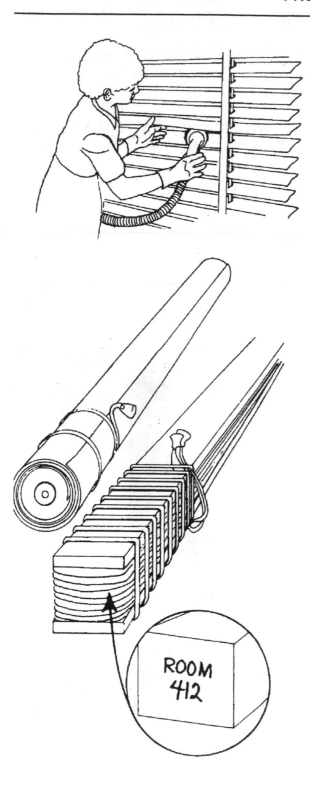

8. Continue this procedure until both panels are completed.

9. Adjust the drapery. Replace ties.

10. Drapery (depending on the type of fabric) is sent out perdiodically to the laundry or dry cleaners. Remove drapes, mark, fold and place in bag. Take to supervisor for cleaning purposes.

11. Clean equipment and return to designated storage area.

- -

Venetian Blinds
(Dusting)

1. Assemble equipment. Take to assigned area. Set up ladder and lock.

2. Lower Venetian blind and place in closed position.

3. Plug in vacuum cleaner. Dust tapes.

4. Start dusting heading (stand on ladder if necessary.) Use side-to-side or left-to-right motion.

5. Dust each slat. Make sure to get behind tapes.

6. Continue this procedure until blind is completed. Dust the other side.

7. Adjust blinds and inspect work.

8. Blind may also be damp dusted by hand.

PROCEDURE

9. Clean equipment and return to designated storage area.

Washing

Blinds may be washed at the window or removed and washed in tub, tank, supersonic machine and/or specialized blind washing equipment. Remember to mark blinds if removed for cleaning.

Washing Blinds by Hand:

1. Assemble equipment. Prepare solution. Take to designated area. Set up ladder and lock. Put on gloves.

2. Lower Venetian blind—vacuum.

3. Place slats horizontal.

4. Wash, rinse and dry tapes.

5. Wash heading. Rinse and dry.

6. Dip cloth in germicidal solution. Wring out. Fold around hand.

7. Take slat in covered hand and use a side-to-side motion—moving left to right, cleaning both sides of the blind at the same time (hold slat with one hand while working with the other hand). Avoid too much water.

8. Rinse and dry.

9. Adjust blinds. Wipe up any spills.

10. Remove equipment. Clean and return to designated storage area.

Wash Away From Window:

1. Assemble equipment. Take to area. Set up ladder and lock. Put on gloves.

2. Remove blinds. Pull blinds to top of frame. Unlock the blind from the frame. Wrap or secure the cord around each end. Mark in an inconspicuous place with indelible marker.

3. Place in cart or on dolly and take to area for washing. The blinds may be hung on special racks for washing and rinse with high pressure unit, or may be scheduled to be washed in the blind louvre washing machine that spray washes and rinses blinds in one operation. Blinds are removed from the machine, hung on racks and allowed to air dry.

4. Pull blinds to top of frames. Wrap or secure cord around each end. Place in cart or on dolly and take back to proper location.

5. Install and adjust blinds.

6. Move equipment. Clean and return to designated storage area.

- - - - - - - - - - - - - - - -

Window Shades

Window shades require periodic dusting, vacuuming and washing. Most shades are washable. Daily dusting can be accomplished while shade is hanging. It may be performed with a damp germicidal cloth or vacuum cleaner or covered broom.

1. Assemble equipment. Take to designated area. Put on gloves.

PROCEDURE

2. Extend shade full length.

3. Vacuum roller—use side to side motion.

4. Vacuum surface of shade. Use up and down motion. Overlap each stroke.

5. Continue this procedure until shade is completed. If very soiled, repeat procedure using side to side motion.

6. Continue to vacuum opposite side—starting at bottom of shade—hold shade with one hand.

7. Vacuum pull edge—use side to side motion.

8. Vacuum surface—use up and down motion.

9. Roll shade clean on cleaned with one hand and continue the dusting procedure until shade is completed.

10. Adjust shade. Inspect work.

11. Clean equipment and return to designated storage area.

12. Report to supervisor any shade needing repair or replacement.

IV. GLASS AND WINDOW CLEANING

PURPOSE: To remove soil, control bacteria, allow passage of natural light and for appearance.

EQUIPMENT:

Utility cart
Ladder (step or platform)
Buckets (two)
Cloths or Sponges or Squeegees
Gloves
Cleaning agents (Trisodium, Vinegar, Clear water, Alcohol, Commercial glass
cleaners, or Synthetic detergents)
Vacuum cleaner
Cloths (lint-free)
Paper Towels

SAFETY PRECAUTIONS:

1. Make sure ladders are in locked position.

2. When using a six-foot or taller step ladder, a second person is required.

3. Place cloth under the bucket to collect spillage.

4. Do not lean out of windows, sit nor stand on window sills or guard rails.

5. Do not place too much water on wooden frames and sashs.

6. Do not wash windows when sun rays are directly on pane.

PROCEDURE

General

1. Assemble equipment, prepare cleaning solution and take to assigned area. Set up as close to work site as possible. (Make sure ladder is on flat surface and is locked and that a cloth is under the bucket to catch spillage.)

2. Prepare window—Remove objects from sill; remove drapery, curtains, shades or blinds, If there are screens or guards, unlock and vacuum.

3. Put on gloves.

4. Vacuum frame and window sills.

5. Wash window frames—starting at top using

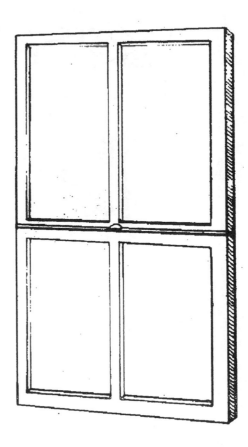

PROCEDURE

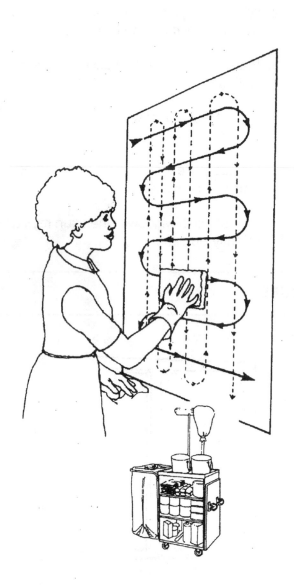

left to right or side to side motion. Then wash the sides using up and down motion.

6. Rinse and dry using same motions.

7. Wash, rinse and dry window sills.

8. Change wash solution, rinse water and cloths. (Clean solution is a necessity.)

9. Dip cloth or sponge into cleaning solution; squeeze out excess water. Start washing at top of window pane (standing to side) using left to right or side to side motion and continue back and forth in one continuous motion until the window is completed. Do not overlook corners. If window panes are very soiled, repeat the washing procedure using up and down motion.

10. Rinse; use the same procedure as washing.

11. Dry with lint-free cloth or paper towel. Use same procedure as for washing. If panes or glass are large or medium in size, use squeegee for drying (using either the "side to side" or "top to bottom" motion) wiping squeegee with cloth after each stroke or when squeegee-pane contact is broken.

12. Continue this procedure until all windows are completed. Then clean equipment and return to designated storage area.

- -

Squeegee Method

1. Apply cleaning solution with sponge or cloth. Use continuous side to side motion.

PROCEDURE

2. Remove water with squeegee. There are two basic motions—*"Side to Side"* and *"Top to Bottom."* Either is acceptable. In the *"Side to Side"* Method, make one continuous stroke starting at bottom of pane with squeegee in flat position and make border. Wipe blade; continue by starting at top of pane (left or right) with squeegee in vertical position; stroke across, and when reaching the opposite side, make a simple half turn overlapping previous stroke. Wipe blade any time squeegee-pane contact is broken. In the *"Top to Bottom"* Method, start at top (left or right corner) of pane and move squeegee to bottom of pane in separate strokes overlapping each stroke. Wipe squeegee blade at the end of each stroke.

3. Wipe up any spills on the sills or frames.

4. Inspect work. Replace items moved from windows and sills.

5. Clean equipment and return to designated storage area.

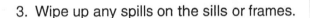

Other Glass Cleaning

Entrance door glass is cleaned daily. Use either the general or the squeegee method. Transoms, partitions and desk tops are cleaned periodically. Use procedure as described in the general method.

V. CLEANING OF LIGHT FIXTURES
(Fluorescent and Globes)

PURPOSE: To control bacteria, assure proper lighting and for appearance.

EQUIPMENT:

Utility cart
Cart on wheels
Ladder (safety or platform)
Buckets (two)
Cloths
Germicidal detergent
Treated cloths
Broom block (with extension handle)
Gloves
Broom bags
Vacuum cleaner/attachments
Screw driver

SAFETY PRECAUTIONS:

1. Always turn off light switch.

2. Schedule when there is least traffic.

3. Do not touch light bulbs while hot or with wet hands.

4. Make sure ladder is locked in position.

5. Do not place fixtures where they can be broken.

6. Move any object interfering with procedure.

PROCEDURE

DRY Fluorescent Light Fixtures

1. Assemble equipment, take to work area. Make sure all lights are off.

2. Move furniture if necessary. Choose either the vacuum cleaner or the covered broom with extension handle.

3. Start at the back of the room. Place cleaning tool against side panel and move forward, using side-to-side motion until you reach the end of the fixture. Then do the other side in the same manner.

4. Continue the process until project is completed.

PROCEDURE

5. Clean equipment and return to storage area. Restock utility cart.

- - - - - - - - - - - - - - - - - - - -

Globes
Incandescent Light Fixtures

1. Take assembled equipment and ladder to work area. Make sure all lights are off.

2. Set up ladder and make sure it is locked. If safety ladder is being used, a second person is required.

3. Put on gloves.

4. Dust light fixtures with treated cloth or damp germicide cloth.

5. Clean equipment and return to storage area. Restock utility cart.

- - - - - - - - - - - - - - - - - - - -

WET
Fluorescent and Globes

1. Assemble equipment in designated work area or utility room and prepare solution for washing.

2. Take ladder and cart to scheduled area.

3. Turn off lights.

4. Remove side panels (lift up and out).

5. Remove louvre (egg crates) loosening one side at a time.

6. Take to designated area.

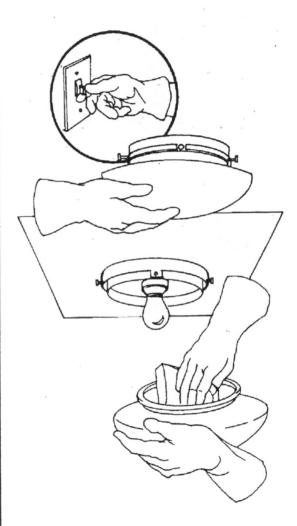

PROCEDURE

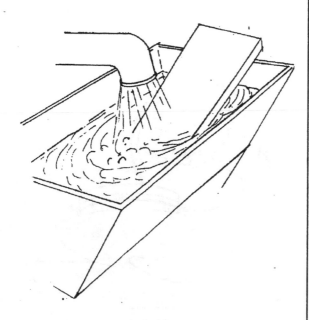

7. Put on gloves.

8. Immerse side panels in prepared solution, wash with soft materials. Don't use any abrasive materials.

9. Rinse in clear water.

10. Dry.

11. Repeat same procedure for "egg crates" and removable incandescent light fixtures (globes). If globes or light fixtures are nonremovable, procedure is to wash, rinse and dry while still attached to the frame.

12. Return light fixtures to their proper area.

13. Attach to frame and make sure that all are securely fastened.

14. Wash and dry all equipment, and return to storage area.

VI. WALL WASHING
(Manual and Machine)

PURPOSE: To remove unsightly soil, control bacteria and for appearance. Walls are also washed for painting purposes.

EQUIPMENT:

Utility cart
Platform ladder or
Step ladder
Cleaning cloths
Gloves
Nylon pad (square)
Drop cloths
Trisodium Phosphate or
Germicidal detergent

Scaffold
Sponges
Buckets (two)
Vacuum (wet and dry or back-pack), and attachments

SAFETY PRECAUTIONS:

1. Areas must be scheduled and the procedure performed when traffic is the least.
2. Secure locking devices on ladder.

PROCEDURE

Manual

1. Assemble equipment. Prepare solution. Take to assigned area.

2. Move furniture to one side of the room or cover it. Remove pictures and other wall mountings. Place in a safe area.

3. Spread drop cloths under portion of wall to be washed.

4. Set up ladder or scaffold. Secure lock if applicable. Put on gloves.

5. If area has not been dusted, vacuum ceiling and walls.

6. Place buckets on cloth on platform (ladder or scaffold).

PROCEDURE

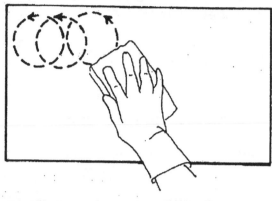

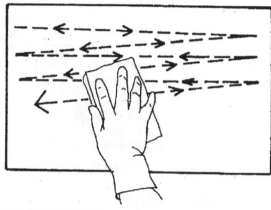

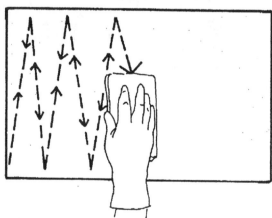

7. Dip sponge into cleaning solution, squeeze out excess water. Take clean cloth to catch drippings.

8. Start at top or bottom. Wash small area. Use circular motion.

9. Dip second sponge into rinse water. Squeeze out excess water. Rinse, use side to side motion.

10. Dry with soft lint-free cloth. Use up and down motion.

11. Continue washing, rinsing and drying until area is completed. Overlap strokes to prevent streaking.

12. Replace furniture. Continue to other side.

13. Move furniture. Continue with the procedure until all walls are washed.

14. Replace all furniture, pictures and mountings.

15. Inspect work.

16. Clean equipment and return to designated storage area.

Machine

The wall washing procedure can be accomplished by machine, thereby saving the institution a great deal of time and labor. The additional equipment necessary to perform this operation includes:

PROCEDURE

Wall washing pressure tanks
Trowels
Wall washing towels
Neutral detergent

SAFETY PRECAUTIONS:

1. Make sure pressure is released before cleaning tanks.

2. Avoid the use of excessive pressure. Excessive pressure will force soil into surface.

1. Assemble equipment. Prepare solution. Take to designated area.

2. Build up pressure in tanks.

3. Place toweling material on trowels.

4. Follow room preparation procedure as in manual wall washing.

5. Dust wall with vacuum.

6. Press solution release levers and thoroughly wet trowels.

7. Begin washing wall. Start by placing trowel in upper corner of wall. Move trowel in a rhythmic side to side motion. Overlap each stroke. Work down the wall by stepping back.

8. Rinse. Use rinse trowel.

9. Dry with third trowel or a clean soft cloth.

10. Continue this procedure until wall is completed.

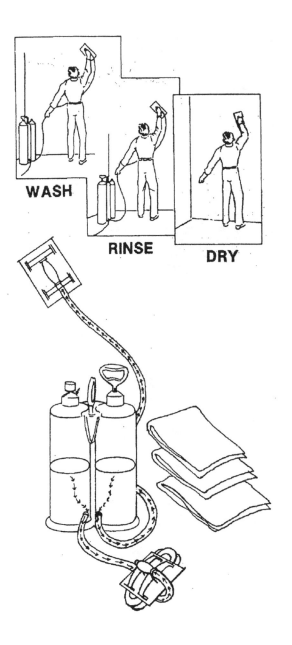

WASH

RINSE   DRY

PROCEDURE

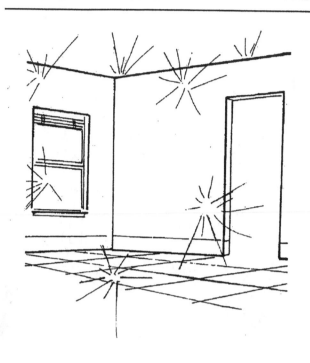

11. Replace furniture and other wall mountings. Inspect work. There should be no streaks, surface contrasts or spots.

Remove towels from trowel and place in plastic liner for laundering. Wash, rinse and dry equipment. Rinse tanks and tubings. Dry. Return equipment to designated storage area.

VII. CLEANING ELEVATOR

PURPOSE: To improve sanitation of the environment, control bacteria and for appearance.

EQUIPMENT:

Utility cart
Counter brush and dustpan
Germicidal detergent
Cloths
Putty knife
Stainless steel cleaner
Electric floor machine
Buckets and Wringers on dolly (two)
Vacuum cleaner (wet and dry)
Four-foot ladder
Gloves
Buckets (two)
Sweeping tool—treated cloth

SAFETY PRECAUTIONS:
1. Take elevator to basement.

2. Put elevator out of order—turn off switch.

3. Do not prop doors open with sticks, buckets, or any other device.

4. Tracks of elevators must be cleaned daily (sometimes more frequently) so that door will open and close properly.

PROCEDURE

1. Assemble all equipment. Prepare solution. Take to designated area.

2. Put on gloves.

3. Vacuum walls, lights, vents, and tracks. Change brushes. Remove gum with putty knife.

4. Vacuum floor or dust with treated cloth.

5. Dip cloth in germicidal solution. Wring out. Spot wash wall areas. Rinse and dry. Wash and dry telephone and box. Wash doors inside and outside. Rinse and dry.

6. Polish all metal surfaces.

PROCEDURE

7. Wet mop floor. Follow wet mopping procedure.

8. Spray buff or buff floor area.

9. Release elevator and continue same procedures until all elevators are completed. Only one elevator should be put out of order at a time.

10. Clean equipment and return to designated storage area.

   NOTE: Once a week, thoroughly clean elevators :
   a. Vacuum thoroughly the walls, ceiling, floors, and tracks.

   b. Wash all walls (interior and exterior), knobs or buttons, control panel, ceiling, vents, ceiling light, telephone, and box. Rinse and dry.

   c. Polish all metal surfaces with recommended polishing agent.

   d. Light scrub floor area.

   e. Apply finish.

   f. Clean all equipment and return to designated storage area.

VIII. ENTRANCE AND LOBBY CLEANING

PURPOSE: to improve sanitation of the environment, to control bacteria and for appearance. The entrance of any building (whether it is a hospital, hotel, home, or business establishment) represents to visitors, potential patients, and others what the interior of the building will be. Therefore, it is very important that these areas are cleaned daily and policed several times each day. The entrance and lobby must be neat and clean at all times.

EQUIPMENT:

Utility cart
Gloves
Cloths or Sponges
Putty knife
Plastic liners/bags
Sifter and slit spoon
Buckets (two)
Electric floor machines
Vacuum cleaner or
Sweeping tool
Glass cleaning agent
Wet floor signs
Buckets and Wringers on dolly (two)
Mopheads and handles (two)
Automatic scrubber
Container for cigarette butts

Squeegee
Spray bottle
Deck brush
Broom and broom bags
Treated cloths
Germicidal detergent
Dustpan and Counter brush

SAFETY PRECAUTIONS:

1. Post wet floor signs.

2. Place equipment near wall area to avoid tripping when not in use.

3. Do not leave electric floor machine unattended and plugged in.

4. Wipe up spills immediately.

5. This operation should be performed during least traffic hours.

6. Clean only half of the lobby at a time. Move furniture.

7. Where urn screens are not in use, use sifter and slit spoon.

PROCEDURE

1. Assemble all equipment. Prepare solution. Take to lobby area.

2. Put on gloves.

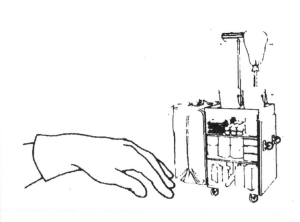

PROCEDURE

3. Clean front entrance. Take broom, counter brush, dustpan and plastic liner to outside area:

   a. Pick up large pieces of trash and place in plastic liner/bag.

   b. Sweep landing and/or steps.

   c. Continue sweeping sidewalk area.

   d. Take up debris with dustpan and counter brush.

4. Return equipment to utility cart.

5. Continue with the cleaning of the lobby:

   a. Post wet floor signs. Move furniture.

   b. Pick up large pieces of trash. Empty trash containers. Wash and dry containers inside and outside. Replace liner.

   c. Empty and wash ashtrays. Clean cigarette urns. Follow urn cleaning procedure.

   d. Take glass cleaning agent and clean cloths or squeegee and wash lobby windows and glass doors inside and outside. Wash any other glass in area at this time. Follow glass cleaning procedure.

   e. Check for cobwebs and remove.

   f. Dip cloth into germicidal solution. Wring out. Damp dust and dry all furniture, window sills, radiators/covers, and other items. Spot wash walls and around light switches. Return cloth frequently to germicidal solution for refreshing.

PROCEDURE

g. Vacuum or dust floor with sweeping tool or covered broom. Make sure to clean runners or mats—vacuum, hose off, mop or scrub.

h. Wet mop floor. Follow wet mopping procedure.

i. Return furniture to proper place and continue with procedure until lobby is completed.

6. Take equipment to utility room. Wash and dry. Return to designated storage area. Restock utility cart.

CAUTION WET FLOOR

STAIRS AND STAIRWELLS,
PORCHES, AND BACK ENTRANCES
(Wet and Dry)

PURPOSE: To maintain a safe and sanitary environment, to control the spread of bacteria, and for appearance.

.

EQUIPMENT:

   Utility cart
   Buckets and Wringers on dolly (two)
   Vacuum cleaner (back-pack or wet and
   dry), or
   Corn broom
   Putty knife
   Germicidal detergent
   Scrub brush
   Gloves
   Mopheads and handles (two)
   Broom bags
   Counter brush
   Wet floor or Out of order signs (two)
   Cloths and Sponges

Buckets (two)
Plastic liner
Deck brush
Dustpan

SAFETY PRECAUTIONS:

1. Report loose treads and banisters and burned out light bulbs.

2. Set up caution signs at *each* doorway.

3. Leave a path open for traffic.

4. When cleaning wide stairs, clean half the width at a time. Leave a dry path for users.

5. Make sure back entrances and stairs are never blocked or cluttered with trash or broken furniture.

PROCEDURE

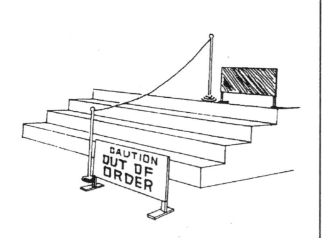

Dry Cleaning

1. Assemble equipment. Prepare solution. Take to assigned area.

2. Place caution sign on the bottom landing.

3. Take second sign, putty knife, and covered broom to top landing.

4. Place sign at top landing.

PROCEDURE

5. Remove any gum. Sweep top landing and work down the stairs. Sweep soil toward closed wall. Use single, continuous, horizontal strokes, and bring down to next step if back of step is closed. However, if back of steps are opened or if steps are opened on each side, counter brush and dustpan are used for this procedure. Sweep each step from both sides to center with counter brush and take up soil in dustpan.

6. Continue procedure until all steps are completed.

7. Sweep bottom landing. Take up trash with counter brush and dustpan. Place in trash bag on utility cart.

8. Dip cloth into germicidal solution. Wring out. Start at bottom and work to top of stairs. Damp dust banister, railing, spindles, radiator, window sills, and ledges.

9. Pick up sign. (Leave sign if wet procedure is being performed.)

10. Continue with the dusting procedure on the opposite side, working down until dusting is completed. (A vacuum may be used to reach difficult areas—ledges, radiators, or to remove cobwebs.)

11. Place caution signs on utility cart. Change cover on broom. Place cover in plastic liner/bag for laundering.

12. Continue to next assignment. If this is the last assignment, clean equipment and return to designated storage area.

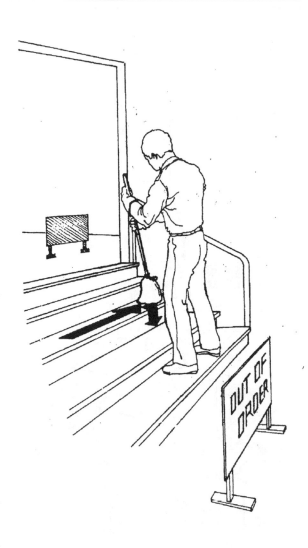

PROCEDURE

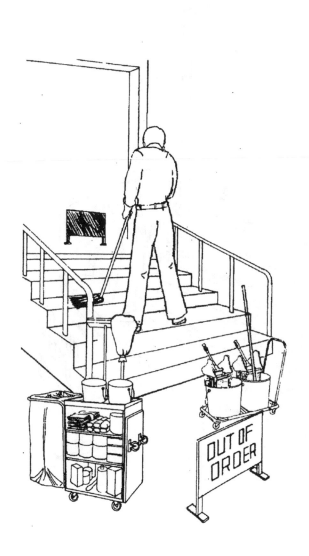

Wet Cleaning
(By Mop)

1. Assemble equipment. Prepare solution. Take to designated area.

2. Sweep stairway with a covered broom.

3. Place buckets on landing. Dip mop into germicidal solution. Press out excess water. Start at top landing and work down.

4. Mop a flight of stairs at a time. Turn mop frequently. Use mop strands to clean corners.

5. Dip second mop into rinse water. Wring out. Pick up soil and solution.

6. Continue this procedure until all steps and landings are completed.

7. Scrub bottom landing thoroughly. Use four-step wet mopping procedure. Apply cleaning solution. Pick up. Apply rinse water and pick up.

8. Take equipment to utility room. Wash, rinse, and dry. Return to designated storage area. Place dust cloths and mopheads in plastic liner/ bag for laundering.

- -

Wet Cleaning
(By Hand)

1. Assemble equipment. Prepare solution. Take to assigned area.

2. Sweep stairway with covered broom.

PROCEDURE

3. Dip sponge into germicidal solution. Squeeze out excess water.

4. Apply solution to treads.

5. Scrub tread with hand scrub brush.

6. Pick up cleaning solution with germicidal solution sponge.

7. Rinse tread. Use second sponge.

8. Pick up rinse water.

9. Continue this process until all treads are completed.

10. Take equipment to utility room. Wash out sponges, brush, and buckets. Return to designated storage area.

Cleaning Wide Stairs
(Dry and Wet)

The procedure for cleaning wide stairs is the same as for narrow stairs with the following changes:

1. Only half of the width of wide steps is cleaned at a time.

2. The dusting procedure is performed before the sweeping procedure.

3. Wide steps are cleaned from bottom up.

USE AND CARE OF
EQUIPMENT, MATERIALS, AND SUPPLIES

CONTENTS

Page

1. GENERAL POINTS TO BE OBSERVED   1

2. USE AND CARE OF NON-AUTOMATIC/MANUAL EQUIPMENT   3

3. USE AND CARE OF AUTOMATIC EQUIPMENT   9

4. HELPFUL SERVICE HINTS FOR WET AND DRY VACUUM   13

5. HELPFUL SERVICE HINTS FOR FLOOR MACHINES   14

6. HELPFUL SERVICE HINTS FOR AUTOMATIC SCRUBBERS   15

USE AND CARE OF
EQUIPMENT, MATERIALS, AND SUPPLIES

1. GENERAL POINTS TO BE OBSERVED:

The institution has invested a large amount of money in expensive modern equipment, materials, and supplies in order to help fulfill the housekeeping goals. Therefore, it is the responsibility of each employee to keep the equipment in good working condition and use materials and supplies economically.

Storing of equipment is part of the Housekeeping Aid's job in caring for equipment. Some institutions have storage areas or utility rooms located in each department or on each floor. Others have central equipment rooms near housekeeper's office. These areas are equipped with hooks, racks, shelves, sinks, and floor drains for the cleaning and storing of equipment, material and supplies.

The storage area must be maintained daily and every item must have a place.

Care of equipment, materials, and supplies are divided into two groups: care of non-automatic/manual equipment, and care of power-operated (electric or battery) equipment. However, there are several general points to be observed on the care and upkeep of all equipment, materials, and supplies.

1. Follow manufacturer's instructions for operation and maintenance.

2. Provide a preventive maintenance program (routine and systematic inspections and repairs).

3. Replace equipment, materials, or supplies promptly when faulty or ineffective.

4. Keep equipment clean at all times.

5. Use materials and supplies economically.

6. Provide adequate and proper storage area for equipment, materials, and supplies.

7. Use each piece of equipment only for its intended purpose.

8. Report faulty, damaged, or ineffective materials or equipment to supervisor.

PURPOSE: To maintain equipment in good working condition; to insure faster, easier, and more efficient performance; to control bacteria and for appearance.

EQUIPMENT:

    Germicidal detergent
    Cloths or Sponges
    Buckets (two)
    Gloves

SAFETY PRECAUTIONS:

1. Never pour used sealer or finish back into clean solution containers.

2. Brushes should never be stored on the bristles or left on machines.

3. Do not use more of an item than is necessary to efficiently perform the task.

4. Make sure pressure is released from wall washing tanks before cleaning.

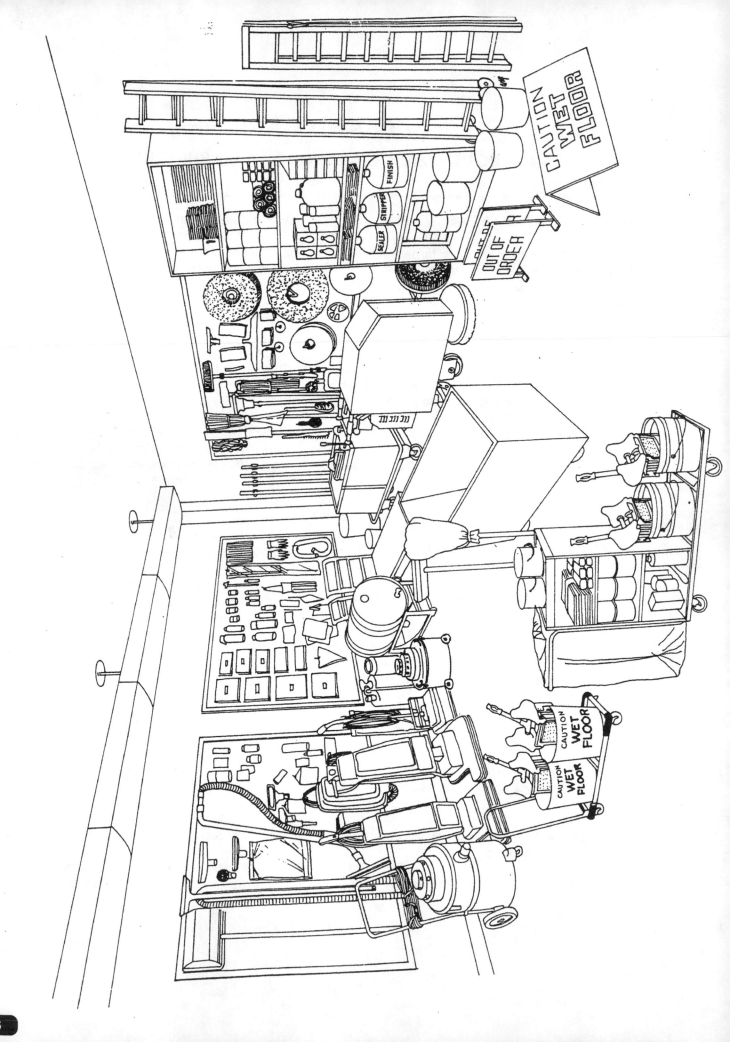

5. All equipment must be cleaned at the end of the day and returned to designated storage area.

2. USE AND CARE OF NON-AUTOMATIC/MANUAL EQUIPMENT:

Included in this type of equipment are items used in housekeeping duties that are entirely moved or operated by hand. This includes everything from brushes to wall washing pressure tanks.

EQUIPMENT:

Utility carts
Brushes of all types:
a. Counter
b. Sweeping
c. Toilet
d. Deck and other Scrub brushes
e. Radiator
f. Scrub and Polish
g. Pot
h. Nylon hand brush
i. Coving or Baseboard

Dustpans
Screens, sifters and slit spoons
Caution signs
Squeegees
Buckets (small and large)
Dollies
Wringers
Mopheads
Nylon pads
Sweeping floor tools
Extension handles
Trash carts
Wall washing pressure tanks
Corn brooms

Ladders
Gloves
Sealers
Strippers (bulk and portioned)
Finishes (bulk and portioned)
Germicidal detergents (bulk and portioned)
Polishes (furniture, stainless steel)
Treated cloths
Dust cloths
Soaps
Plastic liners
Carpet sweepers
Putty knives
Hose (water)
Measuring cups
Mopping tanks
Spray units
Toilet tissue
Paper towels
Bottles (plastic)
Trash containers

PROCEDURE

Utility Carts

1. Wipe off all shelves with germicidal cloth at the end of the day. Dry.

2. Place plastic liner on top shelf to keep from rusting.

3. Use it daily in performing duties as assigned.

4. Keep shelves neatly stocked with all supplies and equipment.

Brushes

1. Clean at the end of the day.

2. Comb with a stiff fiber brush or comb and wash under running water. Shake out excess water.

3. Store by hanging on rack—free from touching any surface or store on block/wood part of brush.

4. Do not use until brushes are dry.

5. For maximum wear and effectiveness, brushes with removable handles should be rotated at least once a week.

6. Always hang broom up. Never stand on the straws.

Bottles
(Plastic spray bottle)

1. Clean exterior with paper towel dipped in germicidal solution. Dry.

2. Return to utility cart.

3. A trigger type must be taken apart regularly and washed and rinsed thoroughly.

Carpet Sweepers

1. Empty into plastic liner after each use. Place liner in trash collection container.

2. Remove strings and debris from brush and wheel.

3. Damp wipe the sweeper.

Caution Signs
(Wet floor, Out of order)

1. Damp wipe and dry after each use.

2. Periodically, thoroughly wash, rinse, and dry.

Cloths
(Treated and Cleaning)

1. Treated:
   a. Use all surfaces of the woven treated paper before discarding.

   b. Treat own cloths by spraying lightly with solution and allow to stand overnight in covered container. May be discarded or laundered.

2. Cleaning:
   a. Rinse frequently during use.

PROCEDURE

---

b. At the end of the day or at the end of the bathroom cleaning procedure, place cleaning cloths in plastic liner, then into a regular laundry bag for laundering.

c. Never leave cloths lying around.

- - - - - - - - - - - - - -

Dustpans

1. Clean at the end of the day. Wash with germicidal solution.

2. Rinse and dry.

3. Hang on hook on cart so that it will not become bent or damaged.

- - - - - - - - - - - - - -

Extension Handles

1. Use as an aid for high dusting.

2. Wipe off daily.

- - - - - - - - - - - - - -

Floor Sweeping Tools

1. Use a disposable cloth.

2. Use all surfaces possible.

3. Damp wipe handle and foot frame daily.

4. Wash tool once a week with germicidal detergent.

5. Hang up on utility cart when not in use.

Germicidal Detergents and Strippers

1. Used in the cleaning operation to remove soil.

2. Do not over use—will destroy flooring surfaces.

3. Use recommended amount only.

4. Read label before using.

- - - - - - - - - - - - - -

Gloves

1. Wash outside of gloves under running water (while on hand) at the end of the day.

2. Remove and wash inside. Wipe dry.

3. Hang across a smooth surface to dry.

- - - - - - - - - - - - - -

Hose
(With cut-off nozzle)

1. Rinse off rubber or plastic hose.

2. Roll in a three-foot circle to prevent kinking. Drain water while rolling.

3. Hang hose on a rack or peg in storage area.

- - - - - - - - - - - - - -

Knives
(Putty—short and long)

1. Wipe handle and blade with germicidal solution at end of day. Dry.

2. Return to cart.

PROCEDURE

Ladders
(Safety and Platform)

1. Wipe off after each use with germicidal solution.

2. Rinse and dry.

3. Return to designated storage area.

Measuring Cups

1. Rinse immediately after use.

2. Dry.

3. Store so that it will not be damaged.

Mops—Dust

1. Do not use to mop up spills.

2. Remove loose soil from mop frequently—by vacuum if possible.

3. Remove mophead at end of day, place in plastic bag and take to designated storage area for laundering.

Mops—Wet

1. Cut off loose and uneven yarn strands.

2. Never twist or squeeze mop extra hard—such action will break fibers and destroy the mophead.

3. Remove mophead at the end of bathroom cleaning and at the end of the day.

4. Place in plastic bag and into laundry bag and take to designated storage area for laundering.

Mopping tanks, Buckets, Wringers and Dollies

1. Remove any loose mophead yarn, string, or foreign matter.

2. Wash, rinse, and dry daily. Invert small and medium size buckets to dry.

3. Keep the equipment in good repair. Report any defects to supervisor.

4. When necessary, add a few drops of oil to casters.

5. Avoid hitting the mopping unit against other objects and walls.

6. Replace bumper strip when needed.

7. Do not allow a cleaning solution to remain in the bucket when the bucket is not in use.

Small Buckets or Pails

1. Empty contents.

2. Wash, rinse, and dry.

3. Turn upside down to dry.

PROCEDURE

Polishes

1. Used on furniture, stainless steel, wood and metal.

2. Use only the recommended amount.

3. It is very annoying to get polish on one's clothes; so, thoroughly rub the surface to remove excess polish.

Paper Towels and Toilet Tissue

1. Replacement supplies.

2. Always place in containers—not in window sills or on top of cabinets.

Screens, Sifters/Slit Spoons

1. Wash and shake off excess water.

2. Dry. Handle so as not to bend screen.

3. Place on hook on utility cart or other designated storage area.

Nylon Pads

1. Wash pads under running water. Rinse.

2. Hang or store on flat surface until dry.

Plastic Liners

1. Used to line trash containers.

2. Must be replaced daily.

3. Do not use for any other purpose than intended.

Sealers, Finishers

1. Items used to protect flooring.

2. These items are very expensive.

3. Use liners in buckets when using sealer and finish.

4. Never pour solution on floor.

5. Wipe up spills or drips immediately.

6. Never waste the product. Pour just enough on mophead in bucket to wet mophead, which should eliminate any material being left over.

7. In case there is a small amount left over—discard it. Do not pour into clean solution—solution will sour.

8. Mopheads should be placed in plastic liner/bag for laundering.

9. Wash, rinse, and dry buckets, wringers, dolly, mops and mop handles used in these operations.

PROCEDURE

Soaps

1. Used for hand washing and bathing.

2. Must rinse before using.

3. Not used for cleaning inanimate surfaces.

Sponges

1. Place in germicidal solution. Wash thoroughly. Squeeze out excess water.

2. Rinse. Squeeze out excess water.

3. Place on flat surface to dry—do not hang on nails.

Squeegees
(Small or large)

1. Wash squeegee blades in germicidal solution.

2. Rinse. Drain off excess water.

3. Wipe dry and return to utility cart or storage area.

4. Do not store with squeegee blades down.

Spray Units

1. Used for spray buffing and dry stripping.

2. Wipe off with germicidal solution.

3. Rinse spray nozzles.

4. Do not let material harden on nozzle.

Trash Containers

1. Used to receive or hold waste.

2. Handle containers so as not to scratch, puncture or bend them.

3. Wipe trash container inside and out daily. Replace liner.

4. Once a month—collect trash containers, take to utility room, and thoroughly wash, rinse and dry or steam clean.

Trash Carts

1. Used for general collection of trash.

2. Take to utility room. Wash inside and outside thoroughly. Let drain.

3. Rinse and let drain.

4. Wipe dry.

Wall Washing Machines/Pressure Tanks

1. Empty at the end of the operation.

2. Rinse tubing and inside of tanks.

3. Wipe off outside with germicidal detergent. Dry.

4. Store in designated storage area.

3. USE AND CARE OF AUTOMATIC EQUIPMENT:

Automatic equipment is equipment that is power operated either by electricity or battery. This type of equipment is very expensive and must be properly maintained to insure good service and maximum efficiency. Therefore, keep this equipment free of dirt, and oiled properly and keep screws and nuts tight. Automatic equipment is usually divided into three categories: floor machines, vacuum cleaners and automatic scrubbers.

EQUIPMENT:

Single disc floor machines—with or without spray attachments
Drive assemblies
Square buffers—Attachments (Plates and baseboard scrubbers)

Shampoo machines
Automatic scrubbing machines
Vacuums

    a. Suction

    b. Back-Pack

    c. Wet and dry

    d. Pile lifter

    e. Upright

Vacuum attachments—wand, hose, crevice tool, brushes—floor, wall, ceiling, upholstery, carpet and attachments for wet floor operation

Battery operated sweepers
Automatic mop assemblies

PROCEDURE

Floor Machines

1. Used for scrubbing, stripping and polishing of large or small areas quickly. Also used for special application—such as spray buffing and dry stripping.

2. Never attach brush by running machine over it and allowing it to lock.

3. Never leave machine unattended. Disconnect when not in use.

4. Machine is cleaned at the end of the day or after completion of assignment.

a. At the work site, tilt machine back on handle. Remove brush and pad or drive assembly and place in plastic liners/bags.

b. Rinse machine in upright position. Damp wipe cord with germicide cloth. Wind cord on handle or storage hooks as it is being wiped. Inspect for defects and report to supervisor.

c. Take equipment to utility room. Remove brushes, pads and/or drive assembly from plastic liners/bags. Wash thoroughly under running water. Store on flat surface or hang on peg to dry. DO NOT

PROCEDURE

USE AGAIN UNTIL DRY.

d. Wash handle and exterior surface of machine. Dry.

e. Tilt on handle and rinse the underside of the brush housing with clean water. Dry.

f. If a solution tank is used—rinse tank and feed lines/tubing. Dry.

g. Store equipment in designated storage area.

h. Never store machines on brushes. Store in tilted position.

- - - - - - - - - - - - - - - - - -

Extension Cords

1. If an extension cord is used, make sure it is the same size as on the equipment so that the proper amount of current is carried to machine.

2. Do not yank on an electric cord to pull the plug from the outlet.

3. Damp wipe cord with germicidal solution. Dry.

4. Wind loosely and hang or lay in a safe place.

- - - - - - - - - - - - - - - - - -

Vacuum Cleaners
(Upright, Wet and Dry, Back-Pack)

1. Used to remove soil from floors and carpeting, window sills, ledges, screens, vents, blinds, upholstery, walls and ceiling; and to pick up water—scrub, rinse, overflow, flooding.

2. Empty upright vacuums when bag is half full
   a. Outer bags may be cloth, mole skin or paper.

   b. Cloth and Moleskin Bags may be vacuumed, but never washed. Discard disposable bags.

   c. Damp wipe handle, hose, and cord with germicidal solution. Dry.

3. Clean wet and dry vacuum at the end of the day.
   a. If used for dry purposes:

   (1) Make sure machine is set up with flannel and paper liners.

   (2) To clean, remove hose, head assembly, and cloth filter. Leave paper filter in place.

   (3) Tilt machine back on handle and wheels. Pull out bag so that it hangs outward.

   (4) Continue raising machine until it is resting on handle. Slap tank several times to dislodge all dirt.

   (5) Remove bag by sliding elastic band off the lip of the tank. Place in a plastic liner. Tie and discard.

   (6) Wash tank inside and outside with germicidal solution. Rinse and dry.

   (7) Wash all attachments. Rinse and dry.

   (8) Wipe off cord and rewind on handle, not around head assembly.

   (9) Wipe off head assembly.

   (10) Check impaction filter. Not necessary to remove after each usage, unless torn, dam-

---

PROCEDURE

---

aged or wet. Supervisor should set a specific time for changing (for example, every 30 days).

(11) Take equipment to designated storage area. Leave head assembly off tank, turn on side for airing and drying purposes.

b. If used for wet purposes:

(1) Make sure machine is set up for the wet operation.

(2) Remove flannel and paper liners and insert the cyclonic separator which has a float that shuts off the suction of the machine when tank is filled to maximum level.

(3) To clean, remove hose, head assembly, and lift out cyclonic separator.

(4) Wheel machine to area with drain or low sink. Tilt tank back on handles to empty. (Some of these have drain valves.)

(5) Rinse two or three times with clean water to remove sludge.

(6) Wash, rinse and dry tank and accessories.

(7) Store in designated storage area.

(8) If impaction filter is wet—allow to dry. Sterilize or autoclave before using again.

— — — — — — — — — — — — — — — — —

Automatic Scrubbers/Sweepers

Used for scrubbing, stripping, buffing, and sweeping large areas. In order for machines to work properly, they must be charged daily in a well ventilated room. Battery must be checked regularly and distilled water added when water is below internal plates or triangle. Battery cover must be left opened when charging. Do not smoke in area when machine is being charged.

1. Automatic Scrubber
   a. To clean, take equipment to utility room. Empty—open dump valve or fold tanks over drain.

   b. Flush tanks, wheels and squeegee. Use a hose to perform this task.

   c. Wash exterior surface with germicidal solution.

   d. Rinse and dry.

   e. Take to designated storage area.

   f. Make sure windows are open.

   g. Report any defects, damages or necessary repairs to supervisor.

2. Powered Sweeper
   a. To clean, take to utility room. Remove and empty trash pan.

   b. Shake down filters—remove and empty pan.

   c. Remove brushes—comb, wash, rinse and shake well. Dry.

   d. Wash exterior surface with germicidal solution. Rinse and dry.

   e. Wash pans. Rinse and dry.

   f. Replace all parts.

   g. Take to designated storage area.

PROCEDURE

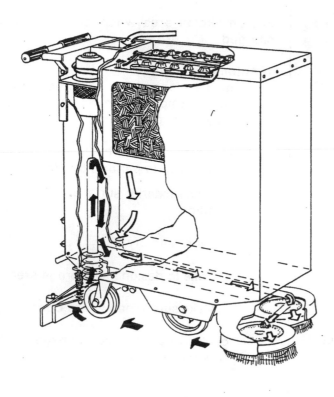

h. Check battery—leave cover open.

i. Connect for charging.

j. Make sure windows are open.

k. Report any defects or necessary repairs to supervisor.

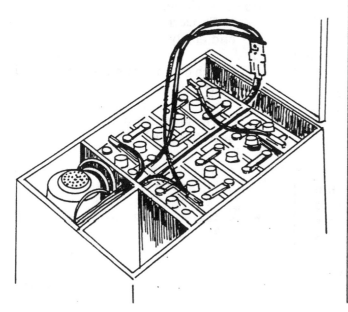

4. HELPFUL SERVICE HINTS FOR WET AND DRY VACUUM:

1. Always operate vacuum on the proper voltages as outlined on the data plate.

2. After using for dry applications, remove the disposable paper bag (5 to 9 gallon units only), and mitten flannel filter and clean before reusing. For added convenience, keep a supply of disposable paper bags on hand (5 and 9 gallon units only)—they may be obtained from your authorized distributor.

.3. If air movement is interrupted in your vacuum, check the dust filter to make sure it's clean. To see if hose has become clogged, remove hose from machine and test suction at machine intake. Sometimes a clogged tool will be the culprit, so check tools periodically.

4. For wet work, remove the disposable paper bag and dust filter, then place the water separator in the tank (5 and 9 gallon units only). In the 10 gallon models, install the wet filter and water shut off.

5. After using machine for wet work, and before putting it away, clean tank inside and outside; clean tools thoroughly.

6. Store machine in clean dry place.

7. The suds supressor bar at the tank inlet should be checked and replaced, if necessary, after 125 gallons of solution have been picked up. Suds supressor bar is replaced by removing inlet deflector and sliding new bar into place. These bars may be obtained from authorized distributor (for 5 and 9 gallon units only).

8. Many tools are available for the wet and dry vacuum. Contact your authorized distributor for additional tools.

SERVICE DIAGNOSIS:

1. Motor will not start
   a. Possible causes:

   (1) Power source or outlet dead

   (2) Vacuum switch faulty or damaged

   (3) Excessively worn brushes

   (4) Wire shorted or broken

   b. How to correct:

   (1) Activate source or check cord

   (2) Replace switch

   (3) Replace brushes

   (4) Replace wires

2. Little or no suction
   a. Possible causes:

   (1) full tank—wet shut off closes fan inlet

   (2) Clogged attachment inlet, hose or vacuum inlet

   (3) Clogged filter bag

   (4) Tank gasket seal leaks

   (5) Exhaust air outlet covered

b. How to correct:

(1) Empty tank

(2) Remove lodged materials

(3) Clean filter bag

(4) Position seal properly

(5) Remove obstruction

3. Machine noisy
   a. Possible causes:

(1) Vibration or resonating of metal parts

(2) Dirty filter

b. How to correct:

(1) Secure all mountings firmly

(2) Clean filter

4. Motor runs hot or smells warm
   a. Possible causes:

(1) Motor cooling air intake or exhaust clogged.

(2) Motor overloaded with mist or suds.

(3) Dirty filter

b. How to correct:

(1) Clean air intake and exhaust passages

(2) Empty tank; install new suds suppressor

(3) Clean filter

5. HELPFUL SERVICE HINTS FOR FLOOR MACHINES:

SERVICE DIAGNOSIS:

1. Machine wobbles—hard to control.
   a. Possible causes:

(1) Brush bristles distorted resulting in brush being uneven

(2) Switch housing not tight on handle tube

(3) Handle tube not connected firmly to machine hose

(4) Pads or brushes worn unevenly

b. How to correct:

(1) If brush is new, soak in water for several hours, remove from water, shake off excess water, rest brush on flat surface on back with bristles pointing upward.

(2) Tighten bolts securing housing to handle tube, tighten set screws. If housing is still loose, drill and tap new hole in housing, insert pointed set screw and tighten firmly.

(3) Check all mounting bolts for tightness, insert washers for shims if necessary.

(4) Replace with new pad or brush.

2. Motor will not run
   a. Possible causes:

(1) Unplugged at wall

(2) Unplugged between motor and handle cable

(3) Fuse blown or circuit breaker tripped

(4) Cable wires severed

(5) Switch burned out

(6) Wires detached at switch

(7) Motor burned out

b. How to correct—follow these steps

(1) Visibly check all connections to be sure the plugs are securely plugged into the appropriate receptacle.

(2) Check fuse or circuit breaker. Replace or reset if necessary.

(3) Visibly, and carefully, check cable for wire breakage.

(4) Unplug motor from handle cable and connect motor directly to wall receptacle through use of an adequate gauge extension cord (at least 14-2). CAUTION: Remove brush or pad holder from machine before plugging into power source.

(5) If after #4 above motor does not operate, remove motor from machine and take it to your distributor, or an electrical repair station designated by your distributor for repairs.

(6) If after #4 above motor does operate, the problem lies between the motor and the wall receptacle. Remove switch box cover plate and ascertain that all electrical connections are secure.

(7) Remove cable from the terminals on the switch and replace with an extension cord (preferably 14-3) to determine if wires have been severed inside the cable.

(8) Replace switch.

3. Runs hot
a. Possible causes:

(1) Motor overloaded. Machine does not have sufficient power for the job. (Example—dry spray-buff cleaning with abrasive pads.)

(2) Air intake ducts clogged with dust and lint.

b. How to correct:

(1) Secure the proper machine for the job or use the same machine with pads of less abrasive material.

(2) Remove drip cover and shroud. Use forced air to blow dust and lint from motor.

6. HELPFUL SERVICE HINTS FOR AUTOMATIC SCRUBBERS:

SERVICE DIAGNOSIS:

1. Motor will not start
a. Possible causes:

(1) Battery charge condition very low—check with hydrometer

(2) Battery connectors loose or disconnected

(3) Loose or broken wires

b. How to correct:

(1) Recharge batteries fully before beginning operations.

(2) Fasten battery connections securely.

(3) Fasten all wires securely and tape.

2. Machine will not move
   a. Possible causes:

   (1) Clutch requires adjusting

   (2) "V" belt slipping

   (3) Battery charge condition very low—check with hydrometer

   b. How to correct:

   (1) Adjust clutch per "Clutch Adjustment" instructions.

   (2) Adjust "V" belt tightness.

   (3) Recharge batteries fully before beginning operations.

3. Machine streaking a cleaned floor
   a. Possible causes:

   (1) Foreign materials lodged under rear squeegee blade

   (2) Insufficient water flow to brushes

   (3) Worn squeegee blades

   (4) Squeegee out of adjustment

   (5) Worn brushes or pads

   b. How to correct:

   (1) Raise squeegee and clean squeegee blade.

   (2) Clean fine filter screen in tank and examine lines for a flow restriction.

   (3) Replace squeegee blade.

   (4) Adjust per instructions.

   (5) Replace brushes or pads.

4. Solution not being properly picked up
   a. Possible causes:

   (1) Vacuum motor wired for 12 or 18 volts and too much solution being laid

   (2) Clogged pick-up tube

   (3) Air leaks around vacuum motor mount

   (4) Ball check (water shut-off) sealing vacuum motor opening to tank

   (5) Clogged filters

   (6) Drain valve not completely closed

   (7) Pick up tube plug or suds suppressors not seated properly

   b. How to correct:

   (1) Use 24-volt switch position.

   (2) Remove lint accumulations and clean tube through plugged hole in tank at top of tube.

   (3) Seal all leaks.

   (4) Clean ball check (water shut-off) assembly and replace.

   (5) Replace filters.

   (6) Close valve.

   (7) Securely seat pick-up tube plug.

5. Short operating time
   a. Possible causes:

   (1) Battery charge condition very low—check with hydrometer

   (2) Continuous heavy motor load due to special brushes

   (3) Constant brush operation—210 lb. position

   b. How to correct:

   (1) Recharge batteries fully before beginning operations.

   (2) Use special brushes requiring heavy motor load only for particular application.

   (3) Use locked brush cleaning operations sparingly.

6. Machine pulls to one side
   a. Possible causes:

   (1) Squeegee dragging only on one side

   b. How to correct:

   (1) Adjust per instructions.

7. Machine creeps
   a. Possible causes:

   (1) Clutch out of proper adjustment

   (2) Clutch cable binding in wound wire casing

   (3) Clutch collar sticking

b. How to correct:

(1) Adjust clutch per "Clutch Adjustment" instructions.

(2) Lubricate clutch cable and casing.

(3) Lubricate clutch.

CPSIA information can be obtained
at www.ICGtesting.com
Printed in the USA
LVHW061550041020
667899LV00006B/79